The Frequent Traveler's Guide

Alexander Anolik
Attorney at Law

&

John K. Hawks
Executive Director
Consumer Travel Rights Center

SPHINX® PUBLISHING
AN IMPRINT OF SOURCEBOOKS, INC.®
NAPERVILLE, ILLINOIS
www.SphinxLegal.com

First Edition: 2005

Published by: **Sphinx® Publishing, An Imprint of Sourcebooks, Inc.®**

Naperville Office
P.O. Box 4410
Naperville, Illinois 60567-4410
630-961-3900
Fax: 630-961-2168
www.sourcebooks.com
www.SphinxLegal.com

This publication is designed to provide accurate and authoritative information in regard
to the subject matter covered. It is sold with the understanding that the publisher is not
engaged in rendering legal, accounting, or other professional service. If legal advice or
other expert assistance is required, the services of a competent professional person
should be sought.
From a Declaration of Principles Jointly Adopted by a Committee of the
American Bar Association and a Committee of Publishers and Associations

This product is not a substitute for legal advice.
Disclaimer required by Texas statutes.

Library of Congress Cataloging-in-Publication Data
Anolik, Alexander.
  The frequent traveler's guide : what smart travelers and travel agents
know.../ Alexander Anolik and John K. Hawks.--
1st ed.
     p. cm.
  ISBN 1-57248-502-7 (pbk. : alk. paper)
  1. Travel. I. Hawks, John K. II. Title.
G151.A55 2005
910'.2'02--dc22
                                        2005030562

Printed and bound in the United States of America.

BG — 10 9 8 7 6 5 4 3 2 1

Acknowledgements

The authors wish to thank the following for their help: Pat Funk and Terri Barger for their support at the Consumer Travel Rights Center headquarters; Phil Cameron and Alex Pevzner in the offices of Alexander Anolik, P.L.C.; Jason Sowards for his essential assistance in legal research; the law libraries at the University of Louisville and the University of Kentucky; Jeff Herman for his invaluable advice; and, most of all, Dianne Wheeler, our editor from Sphinx Publishing, for her limitless patience and enthusiasm for this project. (Did we mention her limitless patience??)

Contents

Introduction

"With knowledge, one can travel the world over.
Without it, it is hard to move an inch."
—*(Chinese proverb)*

Travel defines us as Americans.

From summer vacations in the family minivan to cross-country business trips to quick weekend getaways, we are constantly on the move. Our right to travel has become enshrined in our minds as a basic American freedom. Today, however, the practical realities of traveling have changed tremendously.

The tragedies of September 11—combined with the billion-dollar losses and bankruptcies in the airline industry—have transformed flying into an obstacle course of clogged security lines, shrinking air routes, and confusing changes in airline fees and rules.

Car rental companies now regularly surprise customers with minimum rental rules, airport pick-up charges, and double-digit tax rates. Hotels have frequent guest programs and overbooking policies that rival the airlines in complexity. Traveling overseas now requires ATM cards that work in international bank machines, credit cards that do not tack extra charges onto foreign-currency purchases, and nerves of steel to absorb greater worries about the impact of terrorism and war.

These changes in the travel industry have, in turn, led to a new type of traveler—empowered consumers who want to control their travel experience, prevent unnecessary hassles, save more money, and protect their rights. This book will give you that power in two ways.

1. Teaching you the basics of travel law—what we call Preventive Legal Care—so you can gauge your options and protect your rights as a truly informed traveler (unlike other consumers who rant and rave at service counters without knowing for certain what the travel supplier may or may not owe them).

2. Positioning you with the best arguments, supported by the most current travel law concepts, to defend yourself against travel companies that may be taking advantage of you.

As you read this book, keep in mind these basic *golden rules* for avoiding travel mishaps—and for standing up to defend your rights—when you hit the road.

- *The #1 rule in travel is* caveat emptor—
  Let the buyer beware.
  In the end, you alone hold complete responsibility for protecting your rights as a traveler. You may have selected the most reputable airlines, cruise lines, hotels, car rental companies, tour operators, and other travel suppliers in the world. You may swear by your local neighborhood travel agent, with decades of experience and a Rolodex of industry contacts that takes your breath away. Despite these allies, though, you will almost always bear the burden of speaking up and taking action to protect the investment in your business trip or family vacation.

  The primary precaution is displaying a healthy skepticism about the descriptions, pricing, itinerary arrangements, and other details of your trip. The old saying holds true: If you have been offered a deal that sounds absolutely too good to be true, it probably is.

- *Do your travel homework and always ask questions.*
  When you have a travel offer in hand, use the Internet
  or the local library's reference department to check
  out the details independently. Ask for additional
  quotes on your trip and do not take it for granted that
  you must act immediately in order to *lock in* any special deals or prices. Also, do not assume that the rules
  enforced by one cruise line, for example, are the same
  for competing companies.

  There is no such thing as a stupid travel question.
  If your travel supplier or agent bristles because you
  are asking detailed questions about your trip, take that
  as a red-flag warning. Think twice before you book.

- *Get everything in writing.*
  Many consumers take a simple confirmation letter or
  email as the final word on their travel plans. Instead,
  you must insist on being given the complete details—
  including cancellation procedures and penalties,
  exclusions, warranties, and all other legal disclaimers,
  as well as the trip's dates, times, places, and prices—
  in writing before you sign any check or hand over
  your credit card for deposits or final payments.

- *When a problem occurs, speak up—loudly and often—
  until it is resolved.*
  Remember the adage that *the squeaky wheel gets the
  grease?* Many times, that is the case with travel. There
  are very few well-defined avenues for travelers to follow in pursuing claims or complaints when they have
  problems on the road. Instead, you must be ready to
  complain along a number of different paths, from
  small claims courts to Better Business Bureau offices
  to state attorneys general to the travel company's
  management, in order to reach a resolution.

  By using this book, you can decide whether your
  travel rights have been violated, what specific violations have occurred, and what directions you can take
  to protect yourself.

In the end, empowered travelers make the travel industry an even friendlier place for consumers who want to enjoy their business trips and vacations with few hassles, no hidden charges, and many pleasant memories.

• • • • •

For the very latest updates on travel issues, consult:
www.mytravelrights.com

chapter one:
Air Travel

On September 11, 2001, the World Trade Center tragedy led federal aviation authorities to order the first complete mandatory grounding of all airline flights (even planes still in the air) in U.S. history. Major airlines are still grappling with the aftermath of the terrorism incidents and the resulting financial troubles that have forced several airlines into bankruptcy court. With those historic challenges facing them, though, U.S. airlines have still managed to post an amazing statistic—more than one million Americans take a trip by airplane every single day of the year.

Those passengers face an extremely chaotic array of air carriers, fares, fees, routes, and rules in an industry that is governed by a bewildering mix of federal laws and regulations. (Congress officially deregulated the airlines in 1978, giving up federal control of airline pricing and operations. As a result of deregulation, the airlines are largely exempt from any state statutes or regulations.)

YOUR TICKET

Your airline ticket is a contract between the airline and you. However, you can rarely negotiate any of the contract terms. The contract is written heavily in favor of the airline and some of the terms and conditions governing your flight are often hidden in convoluted legalese. If you look on the back of the typical ticket, you will see fine-print paragraphs called "Conditions of Carriage." Included in these paragraphs is a statement that the airline has filed additional policies with the U.S. Department of Transportation (DOT) about its liability limits and its promised services for passengers. Under federal law, any person who sells airline tickets—including airline employees at the airport or at an airline call center, as well as travel agents, travel websites, and other retailers—must make a copy of the entire contract of carriage (including the statements filed with the DOT) available to you upon request.

The contract of carriage is the basic document governing the relationship between the airline and you. It covers everything from boarding requirements and baggage limits to the compensation you are due if your flight is delayed. While many airlines use similar language in their respective contracts of carriage, there are always important differences as well, so you must always read the actual contract used by your carrier before you file any complaints about your flight.

On domestic flights, your rights are protected by the *Federal Aviation Act*. This act gives the DOT authority to create and enforce regulations governing the responsibilities

Travel Tip

You can also purchase a summary of the contracts of carriage for major carriers by sending $55 for a copy of "United States Air Carriers, Conditions of Carriage, Summary of Incorporated Terms (Domestic Air Transportation)" at:

Air Transport Association
1301 Pennsylvania Avenue, N.W.
Suite 1100
Washington, DC 20004
www.air-transport.org

Know Before You Go

What if you bought a Delta ticket to Paris, but you learn when you board the plane that you will be flying on an Air France jet? Many airlines now have "code share" agreements in which they share flights and passengers. Especially for international trips, you should ask your travel agent or the airline agent if your flight is a code share and, if so, which airlines you will be flying for each part of your ticket.

of airlines and the rights of passengers. While this act preempts most state laws that attempt to regulate airlines, some state statutes and common-law contract rules still apply.

On international flights, your rights fall largely under an international agreement called the *Warsaw Convention*. Almost all of the world's nations that have functional airports now abide by the terms of this treaty. It spells out an airline's liability for any losses you incur because your flight was delayed or your baggage was lost, delayed, or damaged while you are *engaged in international travel*. You meet this qualification if your ticket says that you will be flying between countries that have adopted the Warsaw Convention or if, en route to your final destination, you will stop over in a country that has adopted it.

An interesting wrinkle is that the Warsaw Convention applies based on the way your ticket was issued, not the actual flights. For example, if you have booked a flight from Chicago to Paris, and the flight crashes in Pennsylvania, then you will be covered by the Warsaw Convention because you intended to fly internationally between the USA and France (both nations participate in this treaty). However, if your flight from Philadelphia to Los Angeles veers off course and crashes in Canada, the airline would not be bound by the Warsaw Convention.

E-Tickets

Many travelers now receive electronic tickets (*e-tickets*) when they book a flight. Instead of flight coupons stapled together in a ticket jacket, you are given a six-character *record locator number* and a written receipt or itinerary confirming your purchase (via mail, fax, or email). Always make sure that you receive the written receipt or confirmation notice as soon as possible after you have purchased a flight. You must present this notice when you check in at the airport as proof that you have purchased a ticket; otherwise, you run the risk of delays if the airline's computers are down or if they do not show any record of your reservation.

Ticket Prices

The airlines use complex *yield-management* software to calculate and post millions of different prices for their flights. These airfares can change literally from one minute to the next. They have adopted this practice in an effort to maximize revenues by offering discounts to spur sales on flights with empty seats and, conversely, raising fares to charge the highest prices possible on popular flights. In the end, the passengers on any given flight may have paid wildly different prices for their seats aboard the same airplane—a perfectly legal practice for the airlines, but a constant source of frustration for consumers. For the most part, the airlines are not required to re-ticket you at the lower price if the remaining seats on your flight go on sale after you have already purchased your ticket (and, if they do, you will probably pay a $75–$100 re-ticketing fee in the process).

If you have purchased a *full-fare* ticket—that is, an airline ticket bought at the full retail price, with no discounts at all—then you will face few restrictions on its use. You can return it for a cash refund, trade it for another ticket, or even use it in many cases to switch to a different airline (at its face value). Most full-fare tickets are sold to business travelers and last-minute leisure travelers who are booking trips a few hours or days before departure, after all of the typical advance-purchase discount periods (such as seven-day, fourteen-day, and twenty-one-day advance-purchase fares) have expired.

Tickets purchased at a discount usually carry significant restrictions. They may be *nonrefundable* (you cannot get your money back if you change your mind about the flight), *non-transferable* (you cannot give the ticket with your name on it to another person so that they can take your place), or both. As a very general rule of thumb, the earlier you purchase your ticket, the more likely it is to carry restrictions, whereas many last-minute tickets require you to pay the full fare with no ticketing restrictions. If you are absolutely sure that your travel dates or plans will not change, then buying a discounted ticket that carries restrictions makes good sense. Further, in many cases, you may be able to take a credit for your restricted ticket if you change your travel plans by paying the airline a *change fee* of $25 to $100.

If you must purchase a last-minute airline ticket because of the illness or death of a friend or family member, many airlines offer restricted tickets with *bereavement fares* that can help you avoid paying the full fare. Bereavement policies vary widely among the airlines, so you should check with your travel agent or the airline for complete details. However, be prepared to prove—with a letter from the funeral home, a funeral announcement, or (unfortunately) a copy of the death certificate—that you are flying because a loved one has died.

> ### Travel Tip
>
> With widespread discounts for airline tickets, you may find a better deal than the standard bereavement fare by working with your travel agent or searching the Internet.

LOST TICKET

Each airline enforces different policies when passengers lose their paper tickets. Generally, you must fill out a lost ticket application with the airline. The airline may issue a replacement ticket, but you must sign an agreement that you will pay for the cost of your replacement ticket if someone uses the ticket you have misplaced. Also, you will likely be charged a penalty or service fee for the replacement.

The airline may opt instead to require you to purchase a new ticket at the currently available fare, despite the advance purchase discounts or other savings you may have found when you bought the first ticket. Then, after an extensive waiting period (as long as twelve months), the airline will issue you a refund for the original ticket, if it was not used during that time.

Sometimes, you may lose part of your paper ticket because the airline's gate agent took the wrong coupon when you checked in for one of the flight segments. For example, if you are flying from Miami to Seattle via Atlanta, and the airline agent in Miami takes your Atlanta-Seattle coupon by mistake instead of the Miami-Seattle coupon, you may have trouble checking in for the second segment of your trip. Always check your remaining ticket coupons when you sit down on the airplane, before the flight takes off, to ensure that you have the proper coupons.

As many major airlines continue moving towards the use of e-tickets for most flights, lost paper tickets will become a much less common problem. With electronic tickets, you cannot really *lose* the ticket; if you misplace your printed itinerary or receipt for an electronically ticketed flight, your travel agent or the airline can simply print a new copy for you. However, a growing number of e-tickets go unused every year because travelers forget about the flight or they change their travel plans without reusing the e-ticket in some way. Always keep your e-ticket confirmations and receipts in a single file folder or drawer to keep track of them.

FLIGHT DELAYS, DIVERSIONS, AND CANCELLATIONS

After September 11, it became almost unpatriotic to complain about flight delays, diversions, and cancellations. However, the truth is that long delays and flight changes can cause you significant hardship, especially if you find yourself stuck in an airline lounge (or on the airport floor) for the night. The DOT reports that, in some particularly tough months (with labor strikes or bad weather patterns) as many as one flight in forty has been cancelled, and one in four flights will not arrive on time.

On domestic flights, most airlines include language in their contracts of carriage that spell out the company's responsibilities if a flight is delayed, diverted, or canceled for various reasons. Many of these clauses describe very specifically the reimbursements for your meal and hotel expenses, and some contracts actually list these obligations depending upon your departure airport and your destination airport. They may also offer different benefits based on the cause of the delay or cancellation (for example, more generous terms for mechanical delays than for bad weather). These contract terms are your best bet for recovering your damages and expenses associated with these types of flight problems. Therefore, you should consider printing out this section of the contract of carriage from your airline's website before you leave home.

On international flights, the airline will offer the compensation promised in its contract of carriage, but you will find it difficult to press for additional damages. The Warsaw Convention allows airlines to escape responsibility for damages caused by flight delays if they can show that they took *all necessary measures to avoid the damage* (or that it was impossible to take any measures at all). The airlines have generally won in court with this defense.

OVERBOOKED FLIGHTS

Federal law permits *overbooking* in the airline industry—taking more reservations from travelers than the carrier has available seats. Each year, more than 500,000 passengers lose their seats, voluntarily or involuntarily, as a result of overbooking practices, especially during peak travel times and holiday periods.

If a flight is overbooked, the airline is required by federal regulations to ask for volunteers—passengers who will surrender their seats for a waiting passenger in return for an incentive such as free or discounted airline tickets, frequent flier bonus miles, or even cash. Nine out of ten U.S. passengers who are *bumped* from their seats voluntarily give up those seats in this manner.

If not enough passengers volunteer their seats, then the airline will begin involuntarily *bumping* passengers (usually, travelers who checked in last or who bought their tickets at the latest dates).

To be eligible for *denied boarding compensation*, you must have a confirmed reservation and your aircraft must have at least sixty seats. (Therefore, many commuter flights do not qualify.) On flights within or leaving the U.S.A., the compensation levels vary greatly.

- If your replacement flight arrives at your destination within one hour after the original flight is scheduled to land, you will likely receive no compensation.
- If your replacement flight arrives between one and two hours after the original flight (domestic) or one and four hours (international), you will receive the value of that ticket segment, capped at $200.
- If your replacement flight arrives more than two hours after the original flight (domestic) or after four hours (international), you will receive twice the value of the ticket segment, capped at $400.
- If your original flight included a scheduled stopover of at least four hours, then the airline will owe you additional damages if it cannot get you to either the stopover city or your final destination within the time limits described above.

Travel Tip

If you want to be *bumped* voluntarily if your flight is full, make it a habit to mention that fact to the airline agent when you check in at the airport. You can always negotiate if you feel the incentive offered to you for giving up your seat is not attractive enough.

What if you believe you have suffered damages beyond these amounts (for example, you missed a paid speaking engagement due to being involuntarily bumped, or the bride and groom did not board their honeymoon cruise because their airplane arrived several hours after the ship sailed)? Unfortunately, most airlines protect themselves against such legal claims by including disclaimers within their contracts of carriage specifically waiving any liability for additional damages. By purchasing the airline ticket, you agreed in effect to this waiver, and therefore the chances are slim to none that you could recover your losses through the courts. Your best bet will be appealing to the airline employees at the airport when the incident happens for overnight accommodations, a free ticket, or other benefits in the name of positive customer service.

BAGGAGE

In January 2003, the new *U.S. Transportation Security Administration* (TSA) began screening all checked baggage at every commercial airport (429 of them) in the United States. Also, the war with Iraq led to heightened security checks that may remain in place for some time. In 2005, a growing number of local U.S. airports will resume control of the baggage screening process, substituting privately employed security screeners for the federal TSA screeners. Based on these confusing layers of security procedures, you can avoid trouble before your trip begins if you think carefully about how you pack your bags— and if you know your legal rights in the event that you are questioned or your bags are searched. (Many of the following tips also apply if you are checking in at a cruise port or rail terminal as well as airports.)

Packing Tips

You may carry with you on the airplane two small pieces of luggage—a carry-on bag as well as one *personal item* such as a purse, briefcase, laptop computer case, or camera case. In addition, you can *check* a specific number of suitcases with the airline. (See the *Airline Specifics* at the end of this chapter for each carrier's limits.)

Because federal screeners now screen all checked bags and even open some of them for additional inspections, you should avoid overstuffing your suitcases so that they can easily repack any bag and close it after it has been opened. Put your footwear (shoes, boots, sneakers, etc.) on top of the other contents, and spread out any books and files you are carrying in the suitcase. Never put film in a checked bag, as the latest scanning machines will damage it; instead, put it in your carry-on bag. Place personal items, such as cosmetics or shaving kit contents, in plastic freezer bags so that screeners can view them without losing anything. Write your name, address, and phone number on index cards and place one in each checked bag, along with bag tags on the outside.

Travel Tip

If you are carrying gifts on your trip, do not wrap them before you arrive at the airport, as screeners may have to inspect the gifts when you check in.

Finally, do not lock your suitcases when you check them at the airport, as federal screeners may literally break the locks in order to examine the contents. If they damage your luggage in any way as a result of opening your bags for screening or security reasons—such as breaking a padlock or tearing zippers in the process—the TSA is *not responsible* under current federal regulations for repairing or replacing your suitcases. However, in September 2004, the Transportation Security Administration began settling claims filed by passengers who claimed that their belongings were stolen, lost, or damaged when their checked suitcases were screened at the airport for potential bombs or weapons (the average award: $110).

If TSA screeners do open your bag for inspection, they will place a note inside it telling you that the bag was opened and then reseal it with a *tamper evident* tag. TSA also recommends that you use cable ties purchased at a hardware store in lieu of locks. In the future, TSA will provide special seals that you can attach yourself at the airport.

If you arrive at your destination to find that items are missing from your checked bags after they were inspected by TSA screeners, notify your airline and TSA officials immediately.

Lost or Damaged Baggage

Despite the "war stories" told by many road warriors about problems with airline baggage handling, the truth is that the vast majority of checked bags do arrive on time and in good condition. However, when your luggage has been lost, delayed, damaged, or stolen, you may face serious inconvenience or worse.

New federal regulations have doubled the airline's obligation to pay you (from $1,250 to $2,500 per passenger) if your checked bags on domestic flights do not arrive. However, never pack any item in your checked luggage that you cannot afford to lose. Even though the airline must technically reimburse you for the monetary value of your loss, you may not be able to replace some belongings, such as heirloom jewelry or personal items such as prescription drugs that you must have on your trip.

If your luggage is delayed, the airlines are generally responsible for paying your reasonable expenses that result, such as personal toiletry items. (Many carriers now give *overnight kits* with basic items such as deodorant and shampoo to passengers waiting for delayed luggage.) If you must buy other items, such as a tie for a business meeting that is scheduled before your luggage arrives, keep your receipts and submit a bill to the airline's baggage services agent at the airport for repayment. (On international flights, the Warsaw Convention caps the value of lost or damaged luggage at $9.07 per pound.)

If your bags do not arrive at your destination airport, you should file an immediate claim with the airline's baggage services agent (usually located near the baggage claim area). The agent will enter your claim into the airline's computerized tracking system and issue you a receipt with a toll-free number that you can call once you leave the airport to check

Travel Tip

You can declare a higher value for your luggage when you check in at the airport, but many airlines will assess you a fee for doing so. In these cases, the airline then becomes liable for the higher declared amount. You can avoid airline hassles altogether by shipping your valuables via an overnight delivery service such as FedEx, UPS, or DHL (with the appropriate level of insurance to cover the value) or by using an insurer courier service offered through jewelry stores and other high-end retail outlets.

Know Before You Go

Ever wonder what happens when an airline pays a claim for lost luggage that later turns up? Many carriers sell bags for which they have already paid claims to an Alabama company that in turn sells the luggage contents to the public. You may find great deals on designer clothing, jewelry, and other items at **www.unclaimedbaggage.com**.

on your bags. On the claim form, you should list your belongings as specifically as possible. One excellent strategy to insure that you recover the maximum value of your belongings is to make a packing list before you leave on your trip (or take a quick snapshot of your belongings spread out around your suitcases before you pack them), so that you can later prove that you are telling the truth about your losses.

Guns and other Hazardous Items

Though state and local regulations may permit you to carry a firearm, many airlines have strict rules about carrying a gun in your checked bags (and some airlines do not permit them at all). Therefore, you should always check with your travel agent or the airline for its rules. Firearms carried in checked bags must be unloaded, packed in a locked, hard-sided gun case and declared to the airline when you check in. You may also pack small-arms ammunition in the same gun case (as long as it is not loaded in the gun) or in a fiber, wood, or metal box designed to carry bullets. Guns and ammunition are *never permitted* in your carry-on bags. If you are packing sharp items in your checked bags, such as hunting knives or arrows, they must be properly wrapped and sheathed to avoid injuring TSA screeners inspecting your luggage.

Federal rules also prohibit many hazardous items—such as explosives, fireworks, guns, fuel, and dangerous chemicals—in your checked luggage. Though it surprises many average travelers, it is not uncommon for off-duty police officers and private detectives who carry handguns each workday to forget that they have left a spare sidearm gun in their briefcase or suitcase. Also, some heavy smokers who use old-fashioned Zippo-style lighters may have a spare can of lighter fluid in their shaving kit. Families with children traveling over holiday periods may have packed bottle rockets purchased at home in order to save money when they arrive at their destination.

Before the security upgrades resulting from the September 11 attacks, airport guards would typically confiscate the hazardous item or allow the traveler to take it back to his or her car for storage. These days, however, the discovery of guns, fuel, and other hazards in luggage at an airport checkpoint will almost surely result in major delays, an extremely thorough personal search of the traveler involved, and even arrest and the filing of criminal charges. Federal security agents at airports have no leeway to overlook the traveler's honest mistake or allow the person to take the contraband back to his or her car. If you deal with hazardous items around your home or at your workplace, it will pay to do a quick double-check inspection of your luggage, purse, briefcase, coat or clothing pockets, and any other places in which these items might be mistakenly stored.

On both domestic and international flights, your carry-on bags are also protected under the liability rules if they are damaged, lost, or stolen ($2,500 per passenger on domestic trips, $9.07 per pound for international flights). For example, if you discover upon landing that someone has stolen your cell phone or laptop computer from your bag in the overhead bin, you can submit a claim at the airport to recover your loss. Be prepared to submit receipts or other forms of proof documenting the value of these items.

(See the supplement at the end of this chapter for a complete listing of additional baggage rules.)

Pets

Federal regulations impose strict guidelines on airlines that carry pets. Generally, you may carry a smaller animal in an approved pet carrier aboard the plane as carry-on luggage. However, many airlines do not allow more than one carried-on pet for each flight, so you must tell the travel agent or airline agent about your pet when you reserve your flight.

Pets traveling as checked baggage (on the same flights as their owners) or as cargo (without their owners) fall under the *Animal Welfare Act*. The pet must be at least eight weeks old, fully weaned, and kept in an approved carrier or kennel that meets size, sanitation, ventilation, and capacity standards. The airline must provide water at least once every twelve hours and food every twenty-four hours. You must provide the airline with written instructions on feeding, watering, and administering medications (along with written assurances that you fed and gave water to your pet within four hours of the flight's scheduled departure).

Many airlines have their own pet policies beyond the requirements of the *Animal Welfare Act*. For example, you may be asked to provide an updated certificate of health for your pet. Also, airlines are not required to guarantee that your pet will travel on the same flights that you do, as some smaller airplanes have limited pressurized cargo space and cannot accommodate animals.

If you are traveling with a pet, TSA screeners will conduct a visual inspection of the pet in its carrier. They may ask you to walk through the metal detector with your pet while its carrier is sent through the x-ray machine. Your pet should never be sent through the x-ray machine.

In 2003, the major airlines continued wrangling with the federal government, fighting proposed changes in the rules governing pets on airplanes. Check with your travel agent or the airline for the latest regulations. (See Chapter 10 for additional rules for traveling with pets.)

Permitted and Prohibited Items

The TSA continually updates its official list of items that you can (and cannot) take with you on flights originating within the United States, whether in checked luggage or in carry-on bags. (For the most current list, visit **www.tsa.gov**.) If you are taking a flight originating outside the United States, check with your travel agent or the airline for the applicable rules.

If TSA screeners discover a prohibited item in your bags, they will ask you to get rid of the item immediately by placing it in checked baggage, leaving the security checkpoint with the item, taking the item to your car, or throwing the item away (without any hope of recovering it). In severe cases, such as firearms and explosives, you may actually be detained or arrested, even if you brought the item with you accidentally.

Before you pack, be sure to check the list on the following pages. It can be used as a guideline for your travel preparation.

	In Carry-On Bags	**In Checked Bags**
Personal Items		
Cigar cutters, corkscrews	Yes	Yes
Cuticle cutters, eyeglass repair tools, eyelash curlers, nail clippers, nail files, safety razors, toiletries (e.g., hairspray cans), and tweezers	Yes	Yes
Toys (including robots and guns that are not realistic)	Yes	Yes
Umbrellas	Yes	Yes
Walking canes	Yes	Yes
Medical and Special Needs Devices		
Braille notetaker and related equipment	Yes	Yes
Diabetes equipment and supplies (if properly labeled)	Yes	Yes
Nitroglycerin pills and sprays (if properly labeled)	Yes	Yes
Prosthetic devices and tools	Yes	Yes
Electronic Devices		
Camcorders, camera equipment, laptop computers, mobile phones, pagers, and PDAs	Yes	Yes
Sharp Objects		
Box cutters	No	Yes
Ice axes and ice picks	No	Yes
Knitting and crochet needles	Yes	Yes

	In Carry-On Bags	In Checked Bags
Knives (round-bladed butter or plastic)	Yes	Yes
Knives (other types)	No	Yes
Sabers and swords	No	Yes
Scissors (plastic or metal with blunt tips)	Yes	Yes
Scissors (metal with pointed tips)	No	Yes

Sporting Goods

	In Carry-On Bags	In Checked Bags
Baseballs, basketballs, and soccer balls	Yes	Yes
Baseball and cricket bats	No	Yes
Bows and arrows	No	Yes
Golf clubs	No	Yes
Hockey and lacrosse sticks	No	Yes
Pool cues	No	Yes
Ski poles	No	Yes
Spear guns	No	Yes

Guns and Firearms

	In Carry-On Bags	In Checked Bags
Ammunition	No	Yes
BB/compressed air/pellet guns	No	Yes
Firearms	No	Yes
Flare guns	No	No
Gun lighters	No	No
Gunpowder	No	No
Parts of firearms	No	Yes
Realistic firearm replicas	No	Yes
Starter pistols	No	Yes

	In Carry-On Bags	In Checked Bags
Tools		
Axes and hatchets	No	Yes
Cattle prods	No	Yes
Crowbars	No	Yes
Hammers	No	Yes
Drills	No	Yes
Saws	No	Yes
Screwdrivers	No	Yes
Wrenches, pliers, and other tools	No	Yes
Martial Arts/ Self-Defense Items		
Billy clubs	No	Yes
Black jacks	No	Yes
Brass knuckles	No	Yes
Kubatons	No	Yes
Mace or pepper spray (one 4 fl. oz. container if equipped with safety mechanism)	No	Yes
Martial arts weapons	No	Yes
Night sticks	No	Yes
Nunchakus	No	Yes
Stun guns/shocking devices	No	Yes
Throwing stars	No	Yes
Explosive Materials		
Blasting caps or dynamite	No	No
Fireworks	No	No
Flares in any form	No	No
Hand grenades	No	No
Plastic explosives	No	No

	In Carry-On Bags	**In Checked Bags**
Flammable Materials		
Aerosols (except personal care items)	No	No
Fuels and gasoline	No	No
Gas torches	No	No
Lighter fluid	No	No
Strike-anywhere matches	No	No
Turpentine and paint thinner	No	No
Other Dangerous Items		
Chlorine for pools and spas	No	No
Compressed gas cylinders (including fire extinguishers)	No	No
Liquid bleach	No	No
Spillable batteries (except wheelchair batteries)	No	No
Spray paint	No	No
Tear gas	No	No

TRAVELING WITH AN INFANT

You have several options when you travel with a child under two years of age.

- Hold the infant in your lap during the entire flight (avoiding any extra charges for the child).
- Buy a full-fare ticket for the infant to have a separate seat.
- Buy a half-fare ticket (available from most major airlines) and use a child safety seat that is approved for airline usage.

Check with your travel agent or the airline for complete details on ticketing rules for infants, as each company may have additional restrictions. (Also, read Chapter 10 for the rules on acceptable child safety seats for infants aboard airplanes.)

If you are traveling with children, their carry-on bags (including diaper bags, toys, blankets, strollers, and child safety seats) must go through the x-ray machine. Never leave an infant in any seat or stroller as it passes through the machine. You may not ask the screener to hold your baby or watch a child at any time.

UNACCOMPANIED CHILD

The airlines apply special rules to children five years of age and older who will be traveling without a parent or guardian. These *unaccompanied minors* may be required to purchase nonstop, direct flights to their destination. Along the way, airline personnel will board them before other passengers and escort them off the airplane after everyone else has left. Many airlines also charge additional fees ranging from $25 to $75 or more for any unaccompanied minor. Generally, the airlines charge unaccompanied minors the full adult ticket fare for a given flight.

Parents or guardians checking in and picking up an unaccompanied minor at the airport must follow very strict guidelines for identifying themselves and making the final travel arrangements. The airlines generally assume no special *guardianship* for unaccompanied minors once the trip has ended. (See Chapter 10 for a complete discussion of the issues raised by unaccompanied minors on flights.)

MEDICAL CONCERNS

If you have special medical concerns, alert TSA agents of your needs.

If you expect difficulty in moving around or through the passenger screening checkpoint, you have the right to receive help from TSA screeners in monitoring your carry-on bags as they move through the x-ray machine. They may also help in removing your shoes or helping you to navigate through the checkpoint with a walker, wheelchair, or other mobility device. Crutches, canes, and walkers must go through the x-ray machine. They must be collapsed, if possible, before entering the machine. You have the right to ask for a private inspection of your prosthetic device or body brace.

If you have difficulty hearing, you may ask the screener to write down the information or look directly at you and speak slowly.

If you have a visual disability, you may ask the screener to explain the security process to you, escort you through the checkpoint, perform a hand inspection of your equipment (such as Braille notetakers) if the x-ray machine will damage them, and verbally direct you toward your gate once the inspection is completed. If you use a service animal such as a guide dog, try to carry with you a card or letter confirming the arrangement; screeners are now trained to recognize service animal harnesses and tags. Tell the screener how you must walk through the metal detector with your animal as a team. If the dog's harness or tag sets off an alarm, the screener may perform a hand inspection of these items, but the screener should never remove them from the animal. You should never be asked to leave your service animal for any reason.

Family members or companions traveling with a person who has a hidden disability such as mental illness have the right to advise screeners about the best techniques for touching the person during a pat-down inspection or performing other security measures. Companions, assistants, or family members accompanying a traveler with special needs (or unaccompanied minors) must obtain a gate pass from the airline ticket counter in order to be allowed through the security checkpoint without a ticket or boarding pass.

You should tell the screener if you have diabetes and are carrying supplies (such as insulin) with you. These supplies should be properly labeled showing the name of the medication or the manufacturer's name. If you are wearing an insulin pump, notify screeners before you begin the inspection. If you must carry used syringes in your carry-on bags, they must be kept in a hard, plastic-capped container.

Individuals with pacemakers should ask their doctor for a Pacemaker Identification Card to use when going through airport security. You have the right to ask for a pat-down inspection rather than walking through the metal detector. If you have just had surgery, you have the right to tell the screener where you may be in pain so that the screener will exercise greater care in that area of your body during any pat-down inspection.

You should alert the airline ahead of time if you will be carrying any containers with medical, lifesaving, evidentiary, or scientific items that cannot be opened (as well as crematory urns and containers). You will be asked to provide documentation when you check in for these items, such as a letter from your employer or the funeral home. TSA screeners should not open these containers, if you have followed these guidelines.

If you must travel by air while you are seriously ill—particularly if you require special medical equipment, such as an oxygen tank, or if you travel with an attendant or companion—you should check with your travel agent or the airline for its specific rules governing your medical devices and the airfare paid by your companion. For example, some carriers will assign passengers carrying medical equipment to a specific row or section of the aircraft for easier transfers onto and off the airplane. They may also require you to arrive at the airport at an earlier time than other passengers to give airport agents time to check you in and clear you through the security checkpoint.

If you call the airline directly, tell the reservations agent that you need to speak with an airline official who can give you the company's rules for traveling with the specific type of equipment you will be carrying with you on the flight. (All major U.S. airlines have medical directors or other doctors on staff whose job includes working with passengers who travel with medical equipment.)

(Chapter 10 will explain further the rules governing disabled airline passengers.)

In-Flight Injuries

Despite the threat of terrorist incident, it remains true that you are much safer flying on a commercial airplane than driving your own car. However, passengers sometimes get hurt by falling luggage from the overhead airplane bins, slipping on wet stairs or jetways leading to the airplane, or developing food poisoning from an airline meal.

To claim successfully that the airline holds responsibility for your illness or injury, you must show that the carrier caused the harm due to its negligent or intentional acts. The most common personal injury claim argues that the airline and its employees or agents did not follow federal safety rules, its own internal operations and maintenance rules, or common sense in preventing your illness or injury. For example, one passenger won a multi-million-dollar judgment after suffering a heart attack during a flight when the airline did not follow proper first-aid procedures, did not contact ground authorities for medical help, and did not land at the nearest airport.

Know Before You Go

What if another passenger injures you during a flight? You will have an uphill battle holding the airline responsible, because generally the courts have held airlines liable only for injuries they could have foreseen, caused by events they could have controlled or prevented. For instance, a judge might rule that the airline could have stopped serving alcohol to a passenger who became drunk and then turned violent towards you.

However, the courts do not always agree in airline liability cases. For example, some jurisdictions have held airlines liable for injuries caused by falling overhead luggage, but other courts have reached the opposite conclusion.

On international flights, an airline's liability is capped under the Warsaw Convention at $75,000 for injuries sustained on a flight that begins, ends, or stops in the United States (less in other countries). A recent DOT agreement raised the amount to $139,000 or even the full damages claimed by the passenger. U.S. citizens can now sue international airlines in U.S. courts and apply U.S. personal injury legal standards to the case.

BANKRUPT CARRIERS

Pan Am, Braniff, Eastern, National—the airline industry has lost many famous brand names through the years when these carriers declared bankruptcy or simply stopped flying due to financial problems. Several weeks after 9/11, Congress passed legislation to make permanent a DOT regulation requiring U.S.-based airlines that operate on the same routes as any other airline that declares bankruptcy or ceases operations suddenly to accept that carrier's stranded passengers (on a space-available basis) on their similar flights. The replacement airline may not charge these travelers more than $25 each way in additional fees to transfer them to its flights on the same routes. In December 2004, Congress approved a one-year extension of this rule through the end of 2005.

As another level of protection, you should always use a credit card when purchasing an airline ticket, so that you may request a *charge back* from your bank if the airline goes out of business before you take your trip. (See Chapter 8 for an explanation of the charge back rules.)

DECEPTIVE AIRLINE ADVERTISING

What happens if you open the Sunday newspaper to read a full-page airline advertisement promoting $199 tickets from New York City to Rome—only to call your travel agent a few minutes later to discover that the airline only had two seats on the entire airplane available at that special rate? The truth is, you have little direct recourse against an airline that engages in deceptive advertising—promotions that apply only to a few seats on the flight, bait and switch deals in which the airline tries hard to push you into buying a higher fare than advertised, or major restrictions that get lost in the fine print buried at the bottom of the ad.

Airlines are not bound by state *truth in advertising* laws that crack down on such ads, leaving your primary option to file a written complaint with the DOT. Include the complete details about the deceptive offer and a copy of the ad in question with your complaint with the DOT, but again, remember the saying, *if it sounds to good to be true, it probably is.*

FREQUENT FLIER MILES

What began in the 1980s as a loyalty program for frequent customers has turned into a boondoggle for the airlines. Consumers now hold literally billions of frequent flier miles, especially since major credit card companies began using them as reward points for non-air purchases such as groceries and gasoline. Today, the airlines have taken steps to reduce their liability for these outstanding miles, including new expiration dates on earned miles and programs for trading the miles for magazine subscriptions and floral deliveries.

Many airlines have new formulas changing the standard one air travel mile equals one frequent flier point deal. Now, passengers buying higher-priced full-fare tickets may earn several points per air mile, while travelers holding deeply discounted tickets may earn a fractional point per mile. The fine-print restrictions in frequent flier programs give the airlines wide latitude to change award requirements, limit the number of available seats set aside for award tickets, set expiration dates for the miles, or even cancel the frequent flier system completely without any advance notice or any input from passengers. Again, you will find it difficult to complain under state laws, as the airlines are largely preempted from them, leaving your best option here to sue for breach of contract.

Many carriers also enforce very strict limits on transferring your points or your award tickets to any other person. Some travelers buy, sell, and trade their points and award tickets. You should

Travel Tip

Travelers who have amassed hundreds of thousands of frequent flier miles have tried to pass along the points as part of their wills. Many airlines allow this practice, but they may require proof of death, a specific bequest in the will mentioning the gift of the miles, and a transfer fee to process the changes in their records.

avoid relying on them when you travel, as the airline has the right to confiscate your ticket and deny you the right to complete the flight if you are caught with another person's award ticket. (This regulation does not apply to Southwest Airlines, as it does allow you to exchange or give away your free tickets).

In the past, the Internal Revenue Service attempted to tax the value of frequent flier points earned for business travel as personal income. In audits and interviews with business travelers, for example, the IRS claimed that the travelers should count as additional income the value of any frequent flier award tickets earned from business-related flights but used for personal vacation travel. Because the search for frequent flier tickets used for personal trips proved difficult to track and prove—and because thousands of frequent fliers voiced their disapproval of these claims with their elected officials—the IRS announced in 2002 that it will no longer pursue frequent flier award tickets as personal income for taxpayers.

AIRLINE SPECIFICS

AIRTRAN AIRWAYS
9955 AirTran Boulevard
Orlando, FL 32827
Reservations: 800-247-8726
Customer Relations: 866-247-2428
www.airtran.com

Reservations and Check-In
- Electronic tickets on all flights (paper tickets available only through travel agencies).
- Seat assignments are given at check-in (advance seat assignments on "B," "Y," and "A" fares only).
- Recommended check-in time is 90 minutes before scheduled departure time.
- Boarding deadline is 10 minutes before scheduled departure time.

Baggage
- One carry-on bag per paying passenger (45 inches [height + width + length] maximum), plus one personal item (*i.e.* purse, laptop, or umbrella).
- Three checked bags per paying passenger:
  first checked bag: 70 lbs. and 62 in.
  [height + width + length] maximum;
  additional bags: 70 lbs. and 55 in.
- Excess baggage charge is $50 for each bag after the first three.

ALASKA AIRLINES
P.O. Box 68900
Seattle, WA 98168
Reservations: 800-252-7522
Customer Relations: 206-870-6062
www.alaskaair.com

Reservations and Check-In
- Electronic and paper tickets on all flights ($20 charge for a paper ticket in markets where electronic tickets are available; this change does not apply to paper tickets purchased from travel agencies).
- Seat assignments are given at check-in or through the travel agency.
- Recommended check-in time is 90 minutes before scheduled departure time.
- Boarding deadline is 20 minutes before scheduled departure time.

Baggage
- One carry-on bag per paying passenger (45 inches [height + width + length] maximum), plus one personal item.
- Two checked bags per paying passenger
  (70 lbs. and 62 in.[height + width + length] maximum).
- Excess baggage charge is $50 per piece for one to three excess bags; $75 per piece for four to six excess bags; and, $150 per piece for seven or more excess bags.

ALOHA AIRLINES
P.O. Box 30028
Honolulu, HI 96820
Reservations: 800-367-5250
Customer Relations: 888-771-2855
www.alohaair.com

Reservations and Check-In
- Electronic and paper tickets on all flights.
- Seat assignments are given in advance or at check-in.
- Recommended check-in time is 90 minutes before scheduled departure time.
- Boarding deadline is 15 minutes before scheduled departure time.

Baggage
- One carry-on bag per paying passenger
  (45 inches [height + width + length] maximum),
  plus one personal item.
- Two checked bags per paying passenger
  (50 lbs. and 62 in.[height + width + length] maximum
  for first bag;
  second bag is 50 lbs. and 55 in., maximum).
- Excess baggage charge is $75 per piece for one to three
  excess bags; $100 per piece for four to six excess bags;
  and, $175 per piece for seven or more excess bags.

AMERICAN AIRLINES
P.O. Box 619612 MD 2400
DFW Airport, TX 75261-9612
Reservations: 800-433-7300
Customer Relations: 817-967-2000
www.aa.com

Reservations and Check-In
- Electronic and paper tickets on all flights ($20 charge for a paper ticket in markets where electronic tickets are available; paper tickets in those markets are only available through a travel agent).
- Seat assignments are given in advance or at check-in.
- Recommended check-in time is 90 minutes before scheduled departure time.
- Boarding deadline is 10 minutes before scheduled departure time.

Baggage
- One carry-on bag per paying passenger
  (45 in. [height + width + length] maximum),
  plus one personal item.
- Two checked bags per paying passenger
  (70 lbs.; 62 in. [height + width + length] maximum).
- Overweight baggage charge is $25 per piece (50-70 lbs.);
  $50 per piece (70-100 lbs.).
- Excess baggage charge is $80 per piece for one to three excess bags; $105 per piece for four to six excess bags; and, $180 per piece for seven or more excess bags.

ATA AIRLINES
P.O. Box 51609
Indianapolis, IN 46251-0609
Reservations: 800-435-9282
Customer Relations: 877-617-1139
www.ata.com

Reservations and Check-In

- Electronic and paper tickets on all flights ($20 charge for a paper ticket in markets where electronic tickets are available).
- Seat assignments are given in advance or at check-in.
- Recommended check-in time is 90 minutes before scheduled departure time.
- Boarding deadline is 20 minutes before scheduled departure time.

Baggage

- One carry-on bag per paying passenger
  (45 in. [height + width + length] maximum),
  plus one personal item.
- Two checked bags per paying passenger, or three if the passenger does not have a carry-on bag.
  (First bag: 70 lbs. and 62 in. [height + width + length] maximum;
  second bag: 70 lbs. and 55 in.; third bag: 70 lbs. and 45 in.).
- Excess baggage charge is $75 per piece for one to three ` excess bags; $100 per piece for four to six excess bags; and, $175 per piece for seven or more excess bags.

AMERICA WEST AIRLINES
4000 E. Sky Harbor Boulevard
Phoenix, AZ 85034
Reservations: 800-235-9292 (domestic)
800-363-2597 (international)
Customer Relations: 480-693-6719
www.americawest.com

Reservations and Check-In

- Electronic and paper tickets on all flights; paper tickets can only be issued at an America West ticket office or a travel agency for an additional fee.
- Seat assignments are given in advance or at check-in.
- Recommended check-in time is 90 minutes before scheduled departure time.
- Boarding deadline is 20 minutes before scheduled departure time.

Baggage

- One carry-on bag per paying passenger
  (45 in. [height + width + length] maximum),
  plus one personal item.
- Two checked bags per paying passenger, or three if the passenger does not have a carry-on bag
  (80 lbs. and less than 62 in. [height + width + length] maximum).
- Overweight baggage charge is $50 per piece (51-70 lbs.); $80 per piece (71-100 lbs.).
- Excess baggage charge is $85 per piece after the first three bags.

CONTINENTAL AIRLINES
P.O. Box 4607
Houston, TX 77210-4607
Reservations: 800-523-3273 (domestic)
800-231-0856 (international)
Customer Relations: 800-932-2732
www.continental.com

Reservations and Check-In
- Electronic and paper tickets on all flights ($20 charge for a paper ticket in markets where electronic tickets are available).
- Seat assignments are given in advance or at check-in.
- Recommended check-in time is 90 minutes before scheduled departure time.
- Boarding deadline is 15 minutes before scheduled departure time.

Baggage
- One carry-on bag per paying passenger
  (45 in. [height + width + length] maximum),
  plus one personal item.
- Two checked bags per paying passenger
  (70 lbs. and 62 in. [height + width + length] maximum).
  First Class/Business First/Business Class passengers
  may check an additional bag.
- Overweight baggage charge is $80 per piece (over 62 in., 115 in. max.). In addition, Economy class charges $25 per piece (50-100 lbs.), $50 per piece (71-100 lbs.). OnePass Elite, First Class, and Business charges an additional $50 per piece (70-100 lbs.).
- Excess baggage charge is $80 per piece for one to three excess bags; $105 per piece for four to six excess bags; and, $180 per piece for seven or more excess bags.

DELTA AIRLINES
P.O. Box 20706
Atlanta, GA 30320-6001
Reservations: 800-221-1212 (domestic)
800-241-4141 (international)
Customer Relations: N/A
www.delta.com

Reservations and Check-In

- Electronic and paper tickets on all flights ($10 charge for a paper ticket in markets where electronic tickets are available).
- Seat assignments are given in advance or at check-in.
- Recommended check-in time is 90 minutes before scheduled departure time.
- Boarding deadline is 15 minutes before scheduled departure time.

Baggage

- One carry-on bag per paying passenger
(45 in. [height + width + length] maximum),
plus one personal item.
- Two checked bags per paying passenger, or three if the passenger does not have a carry-on bag
(first bag: 70 lbs. and 62 in. [height + width + length] maximum;
second bag: 70 lbs. and 55 in.; third bag: 70 lbs. and 45 in.).
- Excess baggage charge is $40 for one excess bag; $80 per piece for two to three excess bags; $105 per piece for four to six excess bags; and, $180 per piece for seven or more excess bags.

FRONTIER AIRLINES
7001 Tower Road
Denver, CO 80249-7312
Reservations: 800-432-1359
Customer Relations: 800-265-5505
www.flyfrontier.com

Reservations and Check-In
- Electronic and paper tickets on all flights.
- Seat assignments are given in advance (within 120 days of the flight) or at check-in.
- Recommended check-in time is 90 minutes before scheduled departure time.
- Boarding deadline is 15 minutes before scheduled departure time.

Baggage
- One carry-on bag per paying passenger
  (49 in. [height + width + length] maximum),
  plus one personal item.
- Two checked bags per paying passenger, or three if the passenger does not have a carry-on bag
  (70 lbs. and 62 in. [height + width + length] maximum).
- Excess baggage charge is $75 per piece after the first three bags.

HAWAIIAN AIRLINES
P.O. Box 30008
Honolulu, HI 96820
Reservations: 800-367-5320
Customer Relations: 888-246-8526
www.hawaiianair.com

Reservations and Check-In
- Electronic and paper tickets on all flights.
- Seat assignments are given in advance or at check-in.
- Recommended check-in time is 90 minutes before scheduled departure time.
- Boarding deadline is 15 minutes before scheduled departure time.

Baggage
- One carry-on bag per paying passenger
  (maximum size: 49 in. [height + width + length]),
  plus one personal item.
- Two checked bags per paying passenger
  (70 lbs. and 62 in. [height + width + length] maximum).
- Excess baggage charge is $50 per piece for one to three excess bags; $75 per piece for four to six excess bags; and, $150 per piece for seven or more excess bags.

JETBLUE AIRWAYS
P.O. Box 7435
Salt Lake City, UT 84117-7435
Reservations: 800-538-2583
Customer Relations: N/A
www.jetblue.com

Reservations and Check-In
- Electronic tickets, only, on all flights.
- Seat assignments are given in advance or at check-in.
- Recommended check-in time is 90 minutes before scheduled departure time.
- Boarding deadline is 15 minutes before scheduled departure time.

Baggage
- One carry-on bag per paying passenger
  (45 in. [height + width + length] maximum),
  plus one personal item.
- Three checked bags per paying passenger
  (70 lbs. and 62 in. [height + width + length] maximum).
- Excess baggage charge is $50 per piece after the first three bags. Luggage that exceeds weight and size maximums will be charged $75 per piece.

MIDWEST AIRLINES
6744 South Howell Avenue, HQ-8
Oak Creek, WI 53154
Reservations: 800-452-2022
Customer Relations: N/A
www.midwestairlines.com

Reservations and Check-In
- Electronic and paper tickets on all flights. ($20 charge for paper tickets in markets where electronic tickets are available.)
- Seat assignments are given in advance or at check-in.
- Recommended check-in time is 90 minutes before scheduled departure time.
- Boarding deadline is 15 minutes before scheduled departure time.

Baggage
- One carry-on bag per paying passenger
  (45 in. [height + width + length] maximum),
  plus one personal item.
- Two checked bags per paying passenger, or three if the passenger does not have a carry-on bag
  (first bag: 70 lbs. and 62 in. [height + width + length] maximum;
  second bag: 70 lbs. and 55 in.;
  third bag: 70 lbs. and 45 in.).
- Overweight baggage charge is $50 per piece (50-70 lbs.).
- Excess baggage charge is $25 per piece for one to three excess bags; $50 per piece for four to six excess bags; and, $100 per piece for seven or more excess bags.

NORTHWEST AIRLINES
P.O. Box 1908
Minot, ND 58701
Reservations: 800-225-2525 (domestic)
800-447-4747 (international)
Customer Relations: 701-420-6282
www.nwa.com

Reservations and Check-In

- Electronic and paper tickets on all flights ($25 charge for a paper ticket in markets where electronic tickets are available; $25 charge for converting an electronic ticket into a paper ticket).
- Seat assignments are given in advance or at check-in.
- Recommended check-in time is 90 minutes before scheduled departure time.
- Boarding deadline is 15 minutes before scheduled departure time.

Baggage

- One carry-on bag per paying passenger
  (45 in. [height + width + length] maximum),
  plus one personal item.
- Two checked bags per paying passenger
  (70 lbs. and 62 in. [height + width + length] maximum).
- Overweight baggage is $25 per piece (50-70 lbs.); $50 per piece (71-100 lbs.).
- Excess baggage charge is $80 per piece for one to three excess bags; $105 per piece for four to six excess bags; and, $180 per piece for seven or more excess bags.

SOUTHWEST AIRLINES
P.O. Box 36647
Dallas, TX 75235-1647
Reservations: 800-435-9792
Customer Relations: 214-792-4223
www.southwest.com

Reservations and Check-In
- Electronic and paper tickets on all flights.
- Seat assignments are given in advance or at check-in.
- Recommended check-in time is 90 minutes before scheduled departure time.
- Boarding deadline is 10 minutes before scheduled departure time.

Baggage
- One carry-on bag per paying passenger
  (50 in. [height + width + length] maximum),
  plus one personal item.
- Three checked bags per paying passenger
  (70 lbs. and 62 in. [height + width + length] maximum).
- Excess baggage charge is $40 per piece for one to three excess bags; $60 per piece for four to six excess bags; and, $110 per piece for seven or more excess bags.

SPIRIT AIRLINES
2800 Executive Way
Miramar, FL 33025
Reservations: 800-772-7117
Customer Relations: N/A
www.spiritair.com

Reservations and Check-In
- Electronic tickets, only, on all flights.
- Seat assignments are given in advance or at check-in.
- Recommended check-in time is 90 minutes before scheduled departure time.
- Boarding deadline is 10 minutes before scheduled departure time.

Baggage
- One carry-on bag per paying passenger
    (45 in. [height + width + length] maximum),
    plus one personal item.
- Two checked bags per paying passenger
    (first bag: 70 lbs. and 62 in. [height + width + length] maximum;
    second bag: 70 lbs. and 55 in.).
- Excess baggage charge is $50 per piece after the first three bags.

UNITED AIRLINES
P.O. Box 66100
Chicago, IL 60666-0100
Reservations: 800-864-8331
Customer Relations: 877-228-1327
www.united.com

Reservations and Check-In
- Electronic and paper tickets on all flights ($20 charge for a paper ticket in markets where electronic tickets are available).
- Seat assignments are given in advance or at check-in.
- Recommended check-in time is 90 minutes before scheduled departure time.
- Boarding deadline is 20 minutes before scheduled departure time.

Baggage
- One carry-on bag per paying passenger
  (45 in. [height + width + length] maximum).
- Two checked bags per paying passenger
  (70 lbs. and 62 in. [height + width + length] maximum).
- Overweight baggage is $25 per piece (over 50 lbs.).
- Excess baggage charge is $75 per piece after the first three bags.

US AIRWAYS
P.O. Box 1501
Winston Salem, NC 27102-1501
Reservations: 800-428-4322
Customer Relations: 866-523-5333
www.usairways.com

Reservations and Check-In
- Electronic and paper tickets on all flights ($10 charge for a paper ticket in markets where electronic tickets are available. No charge for paper tickets purchased from travel agencies).
- Seat assignments are given in advance or at check-in.
- Recommended check-in time: 90 minutes before scheduled departure time.
- Boarding deadline is 10 minutes before scheduled departure time.

Baggage
- One carry-on bag per paying passenger
  (45 in. [height + width + length] maximum).
- Two checked bags per paying passenger, or three if the passenger does not have a carry-on bag
  (first bag: 70 lbs. and 62 in. [height + width + length] maximum;
  second bag: 70 lbs. and 55 in.;
  third bag: 70 lbs. and 45 in.).
- Excess baggage charge is $80 per piece for one to three excess bags; $105 per piece for four to six excess bags; and, $180 per piece for seven or more excess bags.

chapter two:
Car Rentals

Since the September 11 attacks, the entire car rental industry continues facing pressures to boost sales to pre-9/11 levels. Therefore, you must be on your guard to navigate stricter reservations policies, hidden service fees, and new contract terms that can trip you up at the rental counter. This chapter details the basic issues involved in renting a car and how to protect your rights if you feel you have been wronged under the car rental agreement.

> ### Travel Tip
>
> Rental car categories vary widely by company and location. The Pontiac Grand Am is a *midsize* car at Alamo, an *intermediate* at Avis, and a *standard* at Enterprise. If you find the same make at a competing company in a lower category, ask your car rental company for a break.

MAKING YOUR CAR RENTAL RESERVATION

When you make a car rental reservation, take time to shop around for the best rental rates and policies. Many companies quote low, daily rental prices that do not include additional surcharges such as local taxes or airport concession and recoupment fees (some of which are not actual taxes, but rather cleverly disguised surcharges to help the company pay facility charges assessed by the airport authority). Also, the lowest rates may come with penalty clauses or other hidden rules that could increase your rental fees significantly by the end of your trip. Most cities around or near airports have locations for several different car rental companies, so be willing to take your business to another company, if you do not like the terms offered by your first choice.

EXTRA CHARGES

When you make a reservation, ask the travel agent or the car rental company representative about all additional charges beyond the basic daily rate, so that you will know the total quoted rental price. You have the right to request this quote in writing.

Specifically, you should ask whether the quoted price contains all fees, taxes, and other charges that might be added to your final price. Also, ask the agent whether the quoted price is *absolutely the lowest price* that is available to you. (If you learn after the rental that a better rate was available, you should contact the car rental company for an adjustment in the price you paid. While the company is not required to make this adjustment, it may do so to keep you as a happy customer.)

Car rental companies set their rates depending on the location of the rental office, the number of days in the rental period (as well as weekends versus weekdays), the travel season, the year and model of the car, and special promotions or discounts (such as frequent flier programs, corporate/association/travel club specials, and credit card rates). Also, some car rental companies have franchise locations that may set their own local rates independently.

PENALTIES FOR EARLY OR LATE RETURNS

Ask the agent for the earliest and latest times you can return the car to avoid any extra charges. Rental car companies generally quote rates that require you to keep a car for a minimum number of days or for a certain part of the week (such as weekends). If you turn in the car early, the company may charge you at a higher rate.

Most rental rates are calculated on a 24-hour basis. In other words, the typical rental day begins at the time you pick up the car and ends 24 hours later. (A car rental *week* usually equals five or more 24-hour days.) Most companies offer a one-hour grace period beyond the end of the rental day, with additional hours at a prorated hourly fee.

However, many companies also assess penalty charges for late vehicle returns, including *extra day* fees that can run as much as 30% or more of the total weekly rate. If you asked for additional services such as insurance, you will likely be charged a full day's coverage, even if you are only a few hours late beyond the rental period. Also, if you rented the car at a special weekly or weekend rate, returning it early or keeping it beyond that special rental period may result in higher rates.

It is generally acceptable for car rental companies to charge these higher rates and penalties if you return your car earlier or later than you promised in your initial rental agreement. However, you should always request a refund or discount if your travel plans changed due to unforeseen circumstances (for example, an unexpected injury or a death in the family), as many companies will consider such adjustments.

MILEAGE CHARGES

Today, unlimited mileage is the standard in most car rental contracts, but you should confirm that when you make your reservation. For example, some companies have added a per-mile fee above a set number of miles in the case of vans, sports utility vehicles, and luxury cars. Also, if you will use the car mainly for local driving, a lower daily or weekly rate with a set number of miles may be cheaper than the standard rates for unlimited mileage.

Know Before You Go

Some car rental firms now charge customers a nominal fee for awarding frequent-flier points on rentals (at Hertz, 50 cents a day, capped at $2 per rental). If you collect these points, ask at the counter about possible additional charges.

AIRPORT RENTAL FEES

City and state governments and airport authorities sometimes add surcharges and taxes directly to car rental rates. Because many car renters are travelers who do not live and vote locally, these fees have become a very popular and painless way to raise funds for tourism promotion, sports stadium construction, and other municipal programs. Some car rental companies also pass along to renters *facility charges* or *access charges* billed to the companies by local airport authorities.

Off-airport rental offices may not be subject to these fees, so their total charges may be lower than airport locations for the same rental car company. Also, you may find that the car rental company charges lower rates to travelers arriving by airplane. If you are making a local pickup at an airport car rental location (instead of arriving on a flight), ask if there is a rate difference.

DRIVER FEES

Many companies assess a fee for any additional persons other than the primary renter who will be driving the car during the rental period. The charge for an additional driver may be a daily surcharge ($5-$10) or a single per-rental charge of $25 or more. California and Nevada specifically prohibit surcharges for additional drivers. Unless the extra driver fee includes additional insurance coverage for you, it is simply additional revenue for the car rental company.

Sometimes, additional driver fees will be waived for your spouse (but not usually your domestic partner), immediate family members, or business associates, as long as they sign the rental contract. However, some local rental offices and franchises may not waive such charges. Also, if the additional driver is not a family member living in the same house as the renter, the other driver must usually provide his or her own credit card for the rental records.

Do not risk violating your rental agreement (and possibly losing your insurance coverage) by allowing another person to drive the rental car without complying with the company's rules for additional drivers. Instead, shop around for a company that charges little or nothing for extra drivers.

In the case of drivers under 25 years of age, many companies assess an extra daily *young driver* surcharge that can run as much as $80. If you fall within this age range, you should definitely ask the rental agent about such surcharges. One effective strategy to avoid such fees is to have an older driver rent the car and list the younger person as an additional driver. Most courts have held these charges not to be discriminatory.

REFUELING CHARGES

Almost every car rental company requires you to return the vehicle with a full tank of gas (or, in a bizarre twist, the exact amount of gas in the tank when the car was picked up). If you forget to fill the tank before returning, or if you are running late and cannot stop to refuel the car, you may be forced to pay an exorbitant price per gallon ($5 or more) for the company to add fuel for you.

You will likely be offered a *fuel plan* option when you reserve the car by which you purchase a full tank of gas at or below local fuel prices when you pick up the car. On the one hand, you nearly always lose money with this option, because you can only break even if you return the car with an empty tank of gas. (Of course, running out of gas on your way to the airport to return a car with the prepaid fuel option can cost you a missed flight.) However, the fuel plan can save you time if you have an early morning flight or if you know that you will be unable to refuel before returning the car.

Sometimes, the company will exclude state and local taxes from the per-gallon fuel price, making it seem less expensive. The company may also add a surcharge simply for adding the fuel or it may charge a minimum number of gallons even though your car needed less actual fuel for a complete fill-up. Always ask at the rental counter for the full details about fuel plan options.

If you refuel the car just before returning it, keep your gas receipt handy to present at the rental counter if you are questioned about refueling.

CHILD SAFETY SEATS

Every U.S. state now requires children under a certain age to be placed in child car seats, even in rental cars. You must bring your own seat or you will be forced to rent one from the car rental company. If you have to rent one, it will usually be at a charge of $5–$15 per day or $50–$75 per week. You may also be asked to place a deposit for the seat rental. You may be charged if you damage or lose the rental seat. Even though it is not always convenient to bring your own seat from home, you may definitely save money.

Some states require seats based on the child's age, the child's weight, and a combination of the two factors. You should always ask the car rental agent when you make your reservation if a suitable child car seat will be available that meets the requirements of the states in which you will be driving.

California and several other jurisdictions require the car rental company to post its child safety seat policies prominently at all rental locations. Do not wait until you arrive at the service counter to check on these regulations.

Many experts recommend the use of metal clips that attach to seatbelts to prevent them from slipping when they hold child car seats in place. Car rental companies do not usually provide these clips, so you should plan to bring your own to be completely safe.

> ### Know Before You Go
>
> Picking up a car from a rental counter in a hotel? Many hotels prohibit these counters from posting signs in their public areas. Be sure the rental agent gives you printed copies of child safety seat rules and other mandatory notices.

VEHICLE DROP-OFF CHARGES

If you rent a car in one location and return it to a different location, car rental companies have different policies governing *vehicle drop-offs*. Some companies absolutely require you to return the car to the original rental location. Others let you return a car anywhere within the same metropolitan area or even the same state at no additional charge.

One-way rentals—picking up the car in one city and dropping it off in a different city—are generally not recommended. When they are allowed, they can bring extra fees as high as $500 or more, in addition to the basic rental charges. Companies have the right to limit their one-way rentals and drop-off allowances to certain car models or rental dates. The car rental locations also have the right to refuse to accept any drop-off cars at all.

Your best strategy may be asking the car rental location if it has a vehicle that needs to be returned to your desired destination. In these cases, the company may waive or reduce drop-off fees.

REPAIR CHARGES

It pays to inspect your vehicle for scratches, dents, and other obvious faults before you leave the rental car lot. You have the right to demand that a company representative acknowledge the preexisting damage in writing on your rental agreement.

At many busy airports, car rental companies do not actually inspect your car for damages immediately upon return. However, you have the right to ask the company's parking lot attendant to inspect your vehicle for damage and sign off on the condition of the car on your copy of the rental agreement before you leave. Keep the signed agreement for your records.

> ### Travel Tip
>
> The major national car rental companies offer free roadside assistance services for their vehicles. If you have a flat tire or other mechanical troubles, call your company's toll-free emergency number to request help.

If the rental car company alleges damage to the vehicle when you return it, you will be charged for the repairs. The exception is if you purchased the loss damage waiver (LDW) when you picked up the car. (See the "Rental Car Insurance" section for details.)

If you believe the repair bill is too expensive, ask the company to provide proof of the actual repair costs (including itemized records for labor and any replacement parts). Compare these expenses to the prices charged by other repair shops in the area. Refuse to pay any bill that exceeds these competing quotes.

> ### Travel Tip
>
> When you inspect a rental car before driving off the lot, make sure the trunk contains an inflated spare tire, a lug wrench, and a jack. Check to see which side of the car the fuel tank door is on. Compare the odometer level to the miles shown on your rental agreement, and confirm that the fuel gauge shows "Full."

If the company charges you for any revenue lost while the car was being repaired, you have the right to demand proof that all of the company's similar cars were rented during this time, forcing the company to turn down rentals. The company must show its actual damages, as well as any exceptions that would have mitigated its losses. If it cannot provide this information, then you have an excellent chance to fight the bill.

RENTAL CAR INSURANCE

Additional insurance coverage sold at the counter means big bucks for car rental companies—more than a billion dollars annually for the industry by some estimates. Many companies actually pay their reservations agents bonuses for selling insurance to travelers. However, the truth is that consumers rarely need complete coverage from the rental company, leading some states to pass laws regulating these insurance sales practices.

To begin, most U.S. drivers already carry auto insurance that provides partial or full protection while driving a rental car (with certain dollar limits and coverage only for rentals within the United States and, sometimes, Canada). Some auto insurance policies only cover cars rented while your own car is being repaired, while others do not cover certain types of vehicles such as luxury cars or vans.

Even though there may be limitations, usually, your personal auto insurance will be the primary source of coverage if you have an accident or suffer an injury while renting a car. Other types of coverage, such as credit card policies and the rental car company's insurance that you may purchase for the rental, will be *subrogated*. This means it will not apply until you have reached the maximum of your own auto insurance coverage. (Your personal auto insurance rates may increase if you file a claim for damaging a rental car.)

Travel Tip

If you have an accident while driving a rental car, remember the basics. Collect the license plate number, driver's license number, and insurance information from the other driver. Request a copy of the police report, call the car rental company, and contact your own insurance agent.

Some states require rental car companies to inform you that their insurance coverage may duplicate your personal auto policy (though these laws do not specify how you must be notified). Your best strategy is talking directly with your auto insurance agent before you rent a car to ask the following questions.

- For what geographical areas does my auto policy offer protection for rental cars? (*Generally, auto policies cover the U.S. and Canada only.*)
- How much liability coverage do I currently have? (*If you own an older car, for example, you may carry only the minimum amount of liability coverage required in your state—a level that may be insufficient to protect you against the risk of completely replacing a brand-new rental vehicle or paying an excessive personal injury claim.*)
- What is the amount of my deductible? (*Are you comfortable with paying that amount out of your pocket if you must file a claim for damaging a rental car?*)
- Does my policy cover only the value of the vehicle listed in my policy? (*If so, then you should compare that value to the replacement cost of the type of car you will usually be renting.*)
- Does my policy cover theft and collision damage? (*Most U.S. drivers already carry collision coverage that can replace the protection sold by rental car companies.*)

Credit Cards

Another potential source of insurance protection is the coverage offered automatically if you pay for your car rental with a credit card. Almost all premium credit cards (*gold cards* and *platinum cards*) offer collision coverage, while many standard cards do not. Very few credit cards of any type offer liability coverage, meaning that their insurance for cardholders will not pay for any damage your rental car may cause to other vehicles, property, or people.

If you plan to rely on any credit card insurance while renting a car, you must decipher the fine print in your cardholder agreement about the limits of this coverage. Some cards cover only certain car rental companies, while others apply only to specific car makes and models. Many cards issued to U.S cardholders do not cover rentals outside the United States. Coverage periods may vary depending on the number of days you will be renting the car and on your reasons for renting (business travel versus a vacation).

If you are judged liable for damage to your rental car, you will be held primarily responsible for paying repair bills and other charges until the credit card company reimburses you for any expenses covered by its insurance provisions. In other words, you may have to carry the bills for several months until the issuing bank sends you a check for repayment. Most credit card coverage for rental cars is *secondary*, meaning that it applies only after other sources of coverage (such as your own car insurance and any protection you have purchased from the car rental company) have been tapped.

To contact your credit card company regarding rental car coverage, call the following:

- *American Express:* 800-528-4800 (standard cards)
  800-327-2177 (gold cards)
  800-525-3355 (platinum cards)
- *Diners Club:* 800-234-6377 (all cards)
- *MasterCard:* Contact your issuing bank
- *Gold MasterCard:* 800-622-7747
- *Visa:* Contact your issuing bank
- *Visa Gold:* 800-847-2911

Many credit card companies specifically exclude coverage for certain types of rental vehicles, including luxury cars, sports utility vehicles, vans, and trucks. Some credit card issuers actually list car model

Know Before You Go

While Diners Club offers primary worldwide coverage for car rentals up to thirty-one days, Discover offers no insurance protection at all.

numbers in their fine print, and others exclude certain types of uses (such as off-road travel or cargo hauling). It pays to take the time to talk to your credit card company to learn the details before you rely on this type of coverage.

Types of Coverage

Rental car companies have various types of insurance policies.

Loss Damage Waiver

In completely technical terms, the *loss damage waiver* (LDW) (also known as the *collision damage waiver* (CDW)) is not insurance, but an agreement by the rental car company that it will pay the bills if the rental car is damaged or stolen while you are using it. In other words, the company shifts the responsibility for collision damages or vehicle loss from you (the standard arrangement in rental car contracts) to the company itself.

Travel Tip

Beware of LDW-style car rental coverage being sold by major online travel agencies like Orbitz ($9 a day). The same caveat about LDW's applies to these plans—you are probably already covered.

LDW's are generally the most expensive form of rental car insurance, with daily charges of $9 to $29 or more. Also, because many rental counter agents receive commissions for selling LDW's, they exert high-pressure sales tactics when you pick up your car to generate additional earnings.

In many cases, LDW's duplicate your own personal auto insurance coverage for car rentals, as well as any credit card coverage you may have. In fact, buying the LDW usually negates any credit card insurance protection for rental cars. However, you should consider purchasing LDW's:

- if you do not have personal auto insurance;
- if your personal coverage levels are not high enough;

- if the car you rent is not covered under your own policy;
- if you are renting a car outside the U.S.; or,
- if you do not wish to be responsible for repair bills until your insurer or credit card company reimburses you for the expenses.

Also, you should be aware that LDW's sometimes include exclusions that may leave you liable for certain types of damages such as a broken window or a torn seat cover. Also, LDW's may be voided:

- if you use the rental car to carry people or property for hire or to tow another vehicle or trailer;
- if you allow an unauthorized person to drive it;
- if you use the vehicle for illegal purposes;
- if you obtain the vehicle from the rental car company under false pretenses;
- if you take the car outside the geographical boundaries mentioned in the rental agreement; or,
- if you damage the vehicle through *misconduct* (such as speeding or driving on unimproved roads).

Beware of high-pressure sales tactics by rental counter agents to convince you to purchase LDW's. For example, some companies train their agents to create doubt in your mind by asking whether you are absolutely convinced that you are covered for any accident or whether you know how much a new car costs to replace. In extreme cases, agents have threatened to deny the car rental, claimed that the traveler will be held in the state until all repair bills are paid if an accident occurs, limited the availability of vehicles, or required additional cash or credit deposits. Report such practices to the attorney general in the state in which you rented the car. You are within your rights to demand a full refund from the rental car company.

Some states have taken extra steps to protect consumers against LDW abuse. For example, California requires rental car companies to disclose to renters the full details of how their

LDW's work compared to the renter's existing insurance plans. However, New York legislators repealed in January 2003 a long-standing ban on selling LDW's in that state.

Personal Accident Insurance

Personal accident insurance (PAI) pays medical and ambulance bills for drivers and passengers in a rental car that result from an accident. You will not typically need PAI coverage if you carry personal car insurance that applies to rental vehicles or if you have health insurance coverage. Always check the specific terms of your existing policies, as well as the list of exclusions in any PAI policy that you purchase from the car rental company.

Personal Effects Coverage

Personal effects coverage (PEC), also called theft insurance, covers your personal belongings if they are lost or damaged due to theft or accident involving the rental car. Generally, PEC policies cover you, your immediate family members, and any additional drivers listed on the rental agreement and their immediate family members as long as the affected individuals are traveling in the car with you.

PEC policies can have so many loopholes that they are rarely worth the expense, especially if you already carry home-owners, renters, or business insurance that protects your belongings. PEC's usually reimburse each person for the cash value of items up to a specified limit (per person and per inci-dent). Many PEC's also include deductibles and exclusions for documents, pets, and more valuable items such as cell phones, computers, cameras, and sporting goods.

Personal Accidents and Effects Insurance

Some companies combine PAI and PEC in a policy called *per-sonal accident and effects insurance* (PAE). If you are offered

PAE, but you need only the PAI or PEC coverage, ask for the single policy at a discount.

Supplementary Liability Insurance Coverage

Liability insurance protects you from the risks of damage caused to other people or property, whereas collision insurance covers only damages to the rental car itself. Car rental companies are chiefly responsible in most states to carry only the minimum levels of liability coverage, as low as $10,000 to $15,000 in some cases. While this coverage may apply to you as part of the standard rental agreement, it is unlikely to help you if you find yourself facing a substantial personal injury lawsuit as a result of a rental car accident.

While LDW's, PAI's, PEC's, PAE's, and most credit card plans do not protect you against liability claims, your personal auto insurance policy (if it applies to rental cars) or your homeowners policy generally does. Talk to your insurance agent, and if your existing policies have liability limits that are too low for comfort, consider increasing those limits. If you rent cars frequently, but you do not own a car, you can purchase a year-round nonowners liability policy from many auto insurers.

Many car rental companies sell supplementary liability insurance policies up to $1 million and beyond in coverage during your rental, but the $7-$9 daily cost does not make sense if you are already covered by your existing insurance plans.

Even if the rental car company provides some level of liability coverage in its standard rental agreement, the coverage is likely the minimum liability level required by state law. This protection may help with minor repairs, but it is unlikely to cover you completely against larger personal injury claims.

If you want more liability insurance protection than the standard rental agreement allows, check your personal auto insurance first. If your personal policy's liability limits are too low for comfort, consider increasing the limit with your auto insurance company. If you rent cars frequently, but you do not own your own car, you can purchase a year-round liability policy from

many auto insurers. Finally, you can purchase supplementary liability insurance directly from the rental car company, but the cost
ranges from $8 to $16 per day for your state's minimum levels.

CANCELING YOUR RESERVATION

When you decide to cancel a rental car reservation, the best
advice is to confirm the cancellation as early as possible—but
definitely before the time and date on which you had agreed to
pick up the rental vehicle. After contacting your travel agent or
the rental car company, ask for (and write down) any cancellation number or code that confirms your cancellation. Also, write
down the name and phone number of the agent with whom you
spoke. These steps will likely protect you in the event that the
rental car company charges a fee for canceling late or for being
a *no show* for your reservation.

Several rental car companies assess charges if you fail to
cancel a reservation before the pick-up time and date or if you
simply fail to show up as
promised. These penalties
range from one day's rental
fees to a $50 charge to the
value of the entire rental. If
you used a credit card to guarantee your reservation, the
company simply charges these
penalties to your card.

Travel Tip

Always ask about cancellation penalties
when you make your initial rental car
reservation, especially if you think there
is a chance you may cancel the trip.

Cancellation and no-show penalties are generally legal if
you received reasonable notice about them when you made the
reservation. If you did not receive such notice, you may challenge the charges. Depending on your situation, the agent's
mention that *other fees may apply* or the listing of such penalties
in the fine print of your rental agreement may not constitute reasonable notice. In these cases, you may dispute the penalty with
your credit card issuer.

OVERBOOK RESERVATIONS

Many rental car companies *overbook* reservations because they know from experience that some renters do not show up to claim their cars. However, this practice sometimes results in a shortage of available cars—even when customers have reservations in advance to pick up vehicles.

If you have a guaranteed reservation for a rental car—generally meaning that you have provided the rental car company your credit card information so that you are obligated to pay the rental fees regardless of whether you show up—then the company must do everything in its power to find you another car from its fleet as a replacement. You will typically receive a car from one of its more expensive rental categories as a *free upgrade*. If this is not possible, the company must help you find a similar car from another car rental firm. If this happens, the company should cover any difference in rates, because your rental agreement offered a car for an agreed-upon price.

Even if you did not guarantee your reservation with a credit card, the rental car company must still do its best to provide the type of car you were promised. The company will likely offer you an upgrade at its expense to a car from a more expensive rental category. If you accept the substitution, you may have agreed to permit the company to change its contract with you; however, you have basically benefited by being assigned a larger, more expensive category of vehicle. If you opt not to accept the upgrade, asking instead for a smaller, cheaper car, the company must offer you an available car at the rate for the lower price category.

Your chances of recovering damages in court if you refuse to accept an available substitute car are minimal. The judge would question why you did not accept the reasonable substitute, particularly if the car offered to you came from a higher rental category.

No Available Cars

In heavy travel seasons, car rental companies sometimes over-book to the point that they literally have no cars available in any categories to give renters who are holding reservations. This sit-uation constitutes a breach of your contract with the rental car company, entitling you to compensatory money damages.

In practical terms, the company should pay you the dif-ference in rates if you have to rent a substitute car from a competing company at a higher rate. If you have sustained damages beyond the difference in rental rates, you should claim compensation from them due to the company's failure to have a car available for you as agreed. Examples include taxi fares and the difference in hotel rates if you had to change to a more expensive hotel in order to be closer to clients because you do not have a rental car. However, these damages must be reasonable and foreseeable. For instance, it would be difficult to file a claim for lost business contracts as a result of the overbooking, since the company will argue that such damages were not foreseeable.

You have the best chances with your claim if the terms of your original reservation include charges if you cancel late or do not show up at all to claim your car. Many judges would conclude that, if this type of language protects the car rental company financially, then it must pay you if it cannot fulfill its promises to you.

UNREASONABLE RESTRICTIONS

Rental car companies have the right to place reasonable limits and conditions on their renters. For example, they may prohibit you from renting a car without a valid driver's license. However, other restrictions (such as being 25 years or older in age) may seem less reasonable. Because you will have almost no chance to negotiate any terms of your rental car agreement, some pro-visions may be unenforceable because they are unfair or you did not receive sufficient notice about them.

Age

Most car rental companies set a minimum rental age at 21 or 25. Some companies will not rent to people under age 25 unless they are traveling on business as an employee of a corporate account or they are members of the armed services traveling on orders. If the companies accept drivers under 25, they usually charge a *young drivers fee*. At the other end of the spectrum, some companies have begun imposing maximum age limits of 70 for renters because senior drivers tend to have a higher risk of serious automobile accidents (due to slower response times or impaired mobility).

Even if you consider yourself to be a very safe driver with a spotless record, these *age discrimination* policies are generally considered legal. In broad terms, rental car companies may set their own rules to do business with whomever they choose, provided that they do not discriminate on the basis of protected civil rights categories such as race or religion. (However, sometimes state law trumps these bans. For example, the state of New York prohibits rental car companies from refusing to rent to drivers 18 years or older based solely on the criterion of age.)

Valid Driver's License

Because all states prohibit operating a vehicle on public roads without a valid driver's license, renters and additional drivers must present a valid license when picking up a vehicle. Your rental agreement will likely be voided and any insurance coverage canceled, if you attempt to use a fake license or if your real one is expired, suspended, revoked, or invalid for any reason.

Credit Card

You must generally provide a major credit card when you reserve a rental car. The car rental company will request a *hold* on your card for an amount slightly larger than the total expected rental charges. This hold may last for several days after you return the car, even after you have paid the full rental charges with your card or in cash.

If you do not have a credit card, you may be required to make a cash deposit against the expected rental bill, or the company may simply refuse to rent to you at all. Though this rule seems unfair to travelers who do not carry credit cards, car rental companies are within their rights to decide the methods by which they wish to be paid.

Driving Record

In many states, rental car companies conduct screenings of your driving record, including reports of drunk driving convictions, speeding and reckless driving tickets, and accidents, in an effort to identify potentially hazardous renters. When you arrive at the rental car counter to pick up a vehicle, the agent will type your license number into the computer to request your record as kept by your state's department of motor vehicles. If your record contains *red flags* that violate the screening criteria of your rental car company, it may refuse to rent a vehicle to you, even if you have a guaranteed reservation.

Generally speaking, rental car companies are most likely to deny you a car if you have any of these common disqualifying offenses or convictions on your driving record:

- speeding tickets or other traffic violations within the past three years;
- any citation for failing to report an accident or leaving the scene of an accident within the past four years;
- any citation for driving a car without insurance or a valid license within the past four years;
- any citation for reckless disregard for life and property within the past four years;
- one or more accidents resulting in an injury or fatality within the past four years;
- a conviction for possessing a stolen vehicle or using a vehicle in a crime, within the past four years; or,

- a conviction for *driving while intoxicated* (DWI) or *driving under the influence* (DUI) within the past six years.

The company should usually advise you if your driving record will be screened when you arrive at the rental counter. (Because they experience so many no shows, car rental companies rarely screen your record when you make your initial reservation.) You have the right to ask the company up front about its specific rental screening standards.

Some consumers complain about screenings because states may not update their motor vehicle databases often and drivers may be blacklisted unfairly for accidents in which they were not at fault. If you believe that your driving record may be questionable, ask your state department of motor vehicles if it makes records available to rental car companies. If it does not, you should be safe. You may also have your driving record evaluated by an independent screening company like TML Information Services (800-743-7891) for

> ### Travel Tip
>
> If you carry your own radar detector to use in the rental car, make sure that it meets the new federal regulations. It cannot use frequencies that disrupt satellite systems or credit-card-enabled gas pumps. Check with your retailer for details relating to your specific product.

approximately $20 or ask your state for a copy of your driving record to see if you have worrisome offenses.

If the rental car company does not screen your record at the time of rental, beware if it asks you instead to sign a pledge affirming that you have no serious offenses on your driving record. In the event of an accident, the company may attempt to shift responsibility to you later by saying that your driving record was indeed not acceptable at the time of rental.

Incidentally, you must obey the same traffic laws in your rental car as every other driver in the state where you are driving. Ignorance is no excuse. If you disobey a quirky local parking ordinance, for example, you are fully responsible even if you did not know the rule.

Also, do not assume that you can dodge tickets because you are driving a rental car. Most rental car agreements specify that you must pay all traffic violations incurred while you rent the car. If you do not pay these tickets, and the rental car company is charged instead, the company will simply bill you for the tickets plus any related fees. If you paid for your rental with a credit card, most companies have given themselves in their rental agreements the right to apply these fees to your card.

Geographical Travel Limits

You may be restricted in the rental agreement from driving the vehicle beyond certain state or national boundaries or into remote areas. One common prohibition is driving a U.S.-based rental car into Canada or Mexico without prior written permission. If you choose to ignore these restrictions, you could face extra charges and the potential loss of your insurance coverage. If you have car trouble or an accident outside your approved driving range, you will likely face higher rental rates and the full responsibility for any repair and towing charges.

Accidents

While car rental companies must use reasonable care to maintain and rent their vehicles, they are not *common carriers*. In other words, they have no meaningful obligation to insure your safety while you are using their car.

Expect a fight if you plan to sue the company for damages or injuries resulting from an accident. The typical rental agreement expressly disclaims warranties of fitness or safety, meaning that the company believes it is not responsible if your vehicle is not safe to operate. However, such disclaimers are routinely disregarded in court, because the rental company occupies a much better position than you to inspect and maintain the car.

Always document any injuries suffered during an accident, preferably with witnesses. Ask the company for a copy of the vehicle's maintenance record. Further, you have the right to refuse to make a statement to any rental company representative or insurance adjuster until you have consulted with your own attorney.

Foreign Rentals

Many countries around the world accept valid U.S. state drivers' licenses with a second form of official identification bearing your photograph. Some nations also require an International Driver's Permit (IDP). (The IDP does not involve any test on your part; rather, it is a form explaining in major languages the type of license you have and its restrictions and expiration date.) You may obtain an IDP for $10 at any AAA (American Automobile Agency) office (take your valid driver's license and two passport-sized photographs).

If you become involved in a traffic violation or accident overseas, police officials may confiscate your license until you have paid any fines and settled claims. Be aware that many European nations routinely use cameras at traffic lights to document speeders and redlight runners. Ask for written receipts as you pay these amounts. If your car rental company is billed for your ticket by local authorities after you have returned the vehicle, the company is within its rights to bill you in turn or to charge your credit card for the amount.

> ### Know Before You Go
>
> Outside the Americas and Europe, expect much stricter guidelines for car rentals. A few nations like China prohibit foreigners from driving vehicles, so many car rentals come with a local driver as well.

Most personal auto insurance policies carry severe restrictions on covering you when you drive in another country. Check with your insurance agent for the details, and be prepared to purchase additional coverage if needed. Some countries like Mexico require you to purchase liability insurance before driving inside their borders, and other nations like Australia and New Zealand require the

Know Before You Go

What about international drivers operating vehicles in the United States? Generally, they must present a valid foreign driver's license plus another photo ID card—preferably a passport—if they wish to rent a car in the U.S.

purchase of car rental company LDW's. (In Europe, some countries require the purchase of theft insurance as a separate policy.)

Very few credit cards offer coverage that applies to international car rentals, and none of them cover rentals in specific locations such as Italy, Australia, and New Zealand.

Keep in mind that it may be very difficult to press any claim against an international car rental company, even if it is a franchised location affiliated with a major U.S. brand name rental firm. The U.S. offices typically claim that they cannot control the actions of their independent overseas franchisees.

A FINAL NOTE

Keep a copy of your completed rental agreement and compare it to the final charges that appear on your credit card statement. Contact the rental car company immediately if there are discrepancies in your charges or if you find *mystery fees* on your statement.

RENTAL CAR SPECIFICS

ADVANTAGE RENT-A-CAR

1343 Hallmark
P.O. Box 5-D
San Antonio, TX 78217-1064
800-777-5500
www.advantagerentacar.com

ALAMO RENT A CAR

200 South Andrews Avenue
Fort Lauderdale, FL 33301
800-462-5266
www.alamo.com

AUTO EUROPE

39 Commercial Street
P.O. Box 7006
Portland, ME 04112
888-223-5555
www.autoeurope.com

AVIS RENT A CAR SYSTEM

6 Sylvan Way
Parsippany, NJ 07054
800-230-4898
www.avis.com

BUDGET RENT A CAR
6 Sylvan Way
Parsippany, NJ   07054
800-527-0700
www.budget.com

DOLLAR RENT A CAR
P.O. Box 33167
Tulsa, OK   74153-1167
800-800-3665
www.dollar.com

ENTERPRISE RENT-A-CAR
600 Corporate Park Drive
St. Louis, MO   63105
800-261-7331
www.enterprise.com

EUROPCAR
1000 Holcomb Woods Parkway
Suite 411 B
Roswell, GA   30076
877-940-6900
www.europcaramericas.com

HERTZ CORPORATION
225 Brae Boulevard
Park Ridge, NJ   07656
800-654-3131
www.hertz.com

NATIONAL CAR RENTAL
208 St. James Avenue
Charleston, SC   29445
800-227-7368
www.nationalcar.com

PAYLESS CAR RENTAL
2350 North 34th Street, North
St. Petersburg, FL   33713
800-729-5377
www.paylesscarrental.com

THRIFTY CAR RENTAL
P.O. Box 35250
Tulsa, OK   74153-0250
800-847-4389
www.thrifty.com

chapter three:
Lodging

When you reserve a room in a hotel, motel, inn, or any form of lodging, you have entered into an agreement that has its roots in the common law of England. In the 1400's and 1500's, travel was a dangerous business. It was almost impossible to make advance reservations and many places of lodging were the only inns within a reasonable distance of each other. Therefore, innkeepers developed a common-law duty to welcome and take care of any person who requested lodging (provided that the property had vacant space). They were regarded as being liable for any harm that might come to guests, their horses, and other property. Though state laws have relaxed this duty as traveling conditions have improved, this *duty to receive* continues to form the basic foundation of every hotel reservation made in the United States.

MAKING YOUR HOTEL RESERVATION

Hotel reservations are simple contracts—the hotel promises to hold a room for your arrival and you agree to pay the room charges. Sometimes, the hotel does not live up to its end of the bargain. You should know your rights if this occurs.

There are two basic types of hotel reservations—guaranteed and confirmed. *Guaranteed* (sometimes called *prepaid*) *reservations* require you to post a means of payment (usually a major

Travel Tip

A quick checklist for hotel reservations.

❑ Guarantee policy?

❑ Cancellation policy?

❑ Check-in and check-out times?

❑ Included meals?

❑ Early departure and late check-out penalties?

❑ Charges for calls and Internet access?

❑ Any local safety concerns?

credit card) when you make the initial call requesting your desired dates and type of room. In return for your guaranteed payment, the hotel agrees to hold a room for you for the entire arrival day, even if you stumble into the hotel lobby at 4 a.m. due to a delayed airline flight. If you fail to show up at all and you did not cancel in advance, you will be charged for the room (either the first night or the entire length of your reservation, depending upon the hotel's policy).

If you have not paid in advance or guaranteed the payment for your hotel reservation, but you have received notice from the hotel that your reservation has been accepted, you are holding a *confirmed reservation*. Even though you have not officially paid for your stay, the hotel must still do its best to provide you a room upon checking in or find comparable lodging if a room is not available.

The exception is if you did not abide by the conditions of the reservation. For example, if the hotel agrees to hold your confirmed reservation until 5 p.m. without a credit card guarantee, and you arrive at the front desk at 6 p.m. because you were stuck in a traffic jam. Then, the hotel has no obligation to hold a room for you or to help you secure a room at another property.

Whether your hotel reservation is guaranteed or confirmed, you should always request a written confirmation (including any confirmation numbers) from the hotel. Have this note handy when you check in.

While the hotel is there to provide you a room, it is within its rights to deny you lodging if it is likely that you will damage the hotel; you will annoy or harm other guests (for example, you arrive at the front desk drunk); or, you will be unable to pay for your room (for instance, your credit card is declined repeatedly upon check-in). If you have already checked into your room and then you fall into one of these categories, the hotel may have the basic right to seek your removal from the room. In extreme situations (for example, you brandish a handgun in the hotel lobby), the hotel may actually have a duty to remove you from its property to avoid liability to the other guests.

> ### Know Before You Go
>
> When you use your frequent guest program points to book a hotel reservation, some chains immediately charge your credit card the amount of a single night's stay plus tax. The charge is refunded to you upon check-out, minus incidentals (such as phone charges). Ask up front when you use your points whether your card will be charged. If you object to this practice, speak to a reservations agent supervisor about a waiver.

OVERBOOKING AND WALKING

Hotels routinely overbook their rooms (accept more reservations than they have available rooms), especially during peak travel seasons or large events, such as conventions. They offer excuses that they must oversell in order to make up for the growing number of travelers who make reservations, but fail to keep them; some guests have not checked out as planned; or, certain rooms require repairs or renovations. Several states now actually impose fines on hotels that regularly overbook. Unlike the airlines, hotels have no right to confirm more rooms than they have available. In essence, they may oversell as they wish with the understanding that they may be held liable for your resulting damages.

In very rare cases, two or more hotels work in concert on *bait and switch* tactics—accepting your overbooking at one hotel so that you can be referred, at your expense, to a more expensive hotel down the street. A share of the revenues are then paid back to the first hotel. If this happens to you, you should file a complaint with the attorney general of the state in which the hotel property is located.

If you have a confirmed or guaranteed reservation, and you have fulfilled all conditions of the reservation (such as arriving on time), the hotel is required to take every reasonable step to take care of you.

Follow these tips to assist getting a room when the hotel has overbooked itself.

- Remain at the front desk and firmly demand your room. (*Do not agree to step aside so that other guests can be checked in, as you then become a less pressing problem for the hotel. Standing your ground increases the chances that the hotel will resolve your problem quickly to avoid a scene.*)
- Ask immediately to speak with the front desk manager or the general manager—someone in authority who can make decisions to take care of you.
- Avoid losing your temper; instead, be polite but persistent. (*Despite the excuses you may be given, the very best question to ask again and again is, "I understand there's an overbooking problem, but what will you do to get me a room right away?"*)
- Do not be afraid to ask for what you want. (*Ask whether more expensive rooms or suites might be available at your guaranteed room rate, or ask to be transferred immediately to a different hotel. The hotel might also provide you with future discounts, restaurant vouchers, gift baskets, or bonus points in its frequent guest program.*) (Always check your credit card statements to insure that you were not charged the higher rates.)
- Let the hotel know that you understand your rights. (*Always write down the names and titles of the hotel staffers who deal with you on the overbooking issue, as well as the specific reasons you were given for why you were overbooked.*)

- Be flexible and creative. (*Ask the manager if he or she has other available options such as staff rooms, rooms that are not yet made up, or even a rollaway bed placed inside a meeting room.*)

Guaranteed reservations give you much stronger rights than confirmed reservations, in that you have literally guaranteed payment for the room. If the hotel does not hold a room for you, it has breached its contract with you and it must take all reasonable steps to secure a similar room for you within the hotel or at a comparable nearby hotel.

The hotel may be required to do the following:

- pay for the first night's lodging at a nearby hotel (called *walking*);
- provide free transportation to the other hotel (or reimburse you for the costs);
- pay the difference in rates (if the other hotel is more expensive) for the remaining nights of your reservation;
- pay for any additional transportation expenses resulting from the move, such as taxi costs if you are beyond walking distance to the convention center in your new hotel); and,
- arrange a long-distance phone call (three minutes) to let your family and your office know where you are now staying, and refer all future incoming calls for you to the other hotel.

Many of these services will not always be offered voluntarily, so be prepared to speak to the highest ranking hotel staffer on duty and to insist (politely, but firmly) on them. If the hotel absolutely refuses to pay these expenses, even though you have a guaranteed reservation, take the names of the hotel employees on duty and keep receipts for all of these expenses so that you can send them to the hotel later for reimbursement.

Call ahead if you are running late to alert the front desk that you will indeed claim your room upon arrival. Mention if you belong to the hotel's frequent guest program (as certain hotel chains give these valued guests additional leeway for late arrivals).

EXTRA HOTEL CHARGES

Beware of hidden charges that many hotels assess on services such as telephone calls, in-room movies, and high-speed Internet access. Some properties charge a daily telephone rental fee regardless of whether you actually use the phone in your room. Other hotels charge a fee for each local call or toll-free call (even the numbers you dial when using your own calling cards) or an Internet access surcharge on calls that last longer than thirty minutes.

The worst hotel telephone surcharges are added to long-distance calls made directly from your room phone—three to six times the typical calling card fees for such calls. One national hotel consulting firm estimates that phone fees alone make up 2% to 3% of the average hotel's revenues.

Always ask about the details of any additional phone or entertainment charges when you check in. For example, if the hotel gives guests free local calls, *local* may mean only certain exchanges in major metropolitan areas. Many states now require hotels to post a notice of these fees in rooms, but the notices may not always be prominent.

One craze that has passed its prime is tacking an energy surcharge of $1.50 to $4 a day onto hotel bills to help owners pay soaring electricity bills. Many chains that initially added the fees removed them after guests filed lawsuits and complained to state attorneys general.

If you are charged upon checking out for phone calls, movies, or other services that

Travel Tip

MasterCard International recently overturned a long-standing policy that cardholders may claim hotels charged them wrongly without having to prove it. Now, hotels can dispute these chargebacks. If you encounter problems at a hotel, always keep any receipts or documentation, including the names of hotel staffers with whom you dealt, so that you can press your case.

you did not incur, immediately ask the front desk clerk to remove them from your bill before you pay for your stay.

OTHER FEES

To increase their revenues and control their inventory, many hotels have begun cracking down on guests who do not show up as promised, who cancel their reservations late, or who leave the hotel earlier than expected.

In the past, the rule of thumb to avoid *no show* and *cancellation penalties* was contacting the hotel by 6 p.m. on the day of arrival. However, about a third of hotels—particularly downtown hotels and popular resorts in cities like Orlando and Las Vegas—now require notice 24 hours before the expected arrival. Around 10% of hotels now charge at least the first night's room rate if you do not cancel 48 hours to 72 hours ahead of time.

If you reserve a stay of several nights at a hotel (especially the major chains), but you decide to depart earlier than expected, you may be assessed an *early departure fee* of $50-$100 because you did not stay for the entire length of reserved time. About 15% of U.S. hotels (mostly hotel chain properties in larger cities) now charge this type of fee.

Know Before You Go

If you must cancel your trip due to a hurricane or other severe weather, can you request a refund on hotel deposits? It depends on the hotel. Many hotels in hurricane-prone areas, like the Carolinas and the Caribbean, will work with you if you call in advance (rather than simply not showing up at all).

If you leave your room after the posted check-out time (typically 12 noon to 3 p.m.), some chains like Hyatt, Starwood, and Wyndham may charge up to 50% of the daily room rate as a *late check-out fee*.

These policies sometimes depend on the type of room rate you have booked. Heavily discounted rates offered on travel websites often carry the most onerous cancellation penalties.

Always ask your travel agent or the hotel for its current policies on cancellations and early departures (and request a written copy for added peace of mind). These rules may vary greatly depending on the travel season, and two hotels in the same chain may enforce very different policies.

THE ROOM

Fundamentally, your hotel room—its size, condition, location, comfort, amenities, furnishings, and other factors—should reflect fairly the price charged by the hotel and paid by you as the guest. However, keep in mind that the rate for a room can change dramatically based on any number of factors. Hotels start with a *rack rate*—the maximum that a hotel charges for a single night—and then applies any discounts offered or requested. Offered discounts may include corporate rate, weekend rate, multinight stay, frequent guest rate and a variety of other discounts to get your business. Other discounts you may have to ask for such as AAA, AARP, special group rate, or one you negotiate on the spot.

Travel Tip

If you plan to attend a wedding or family reunion, but the hotel's *special group rate* is already sold out, don't worry. Experts say you can usually do better on your own, as room reservations open up closer to the date of the event. Your best bet is calling the hotel and asking for a room at the very best rate and asking for any available discounts.

Negotiating the rate can be done in person, over the telephone, or online. Each of these methods can result in a different price quote. Several leading hotel chains, notably Six Continents (Holiday Inn, Crowne Plaza, Inter-Continental), Starwood (Westin, Sheraton), and Cendant (Ramada Inn, Howard Johnson), now offer Web price guarantees. They will beat any price you find you find on other travel websites if you book the room through their own sites. If you book online, do not be afraid to try to negotiate the price when you arrive at the hotel—you may be able to lower the price even more.

In addition to pricing their rooms, hotels have some latitude to describe their properties and rooms in positive terms in their advertising and promotions. However, a hotel may be guilty of fraud or deception if its ads intentionally misrepresent what you will receive in return for your room rate. The most common complaints arise regarding the hotel's (or room's) location and condition.

If you believe you have been misled about the location of your room—for example, the promised *garden view* is actually the dumpster behind the hotel's kitchens—talk to the front desk manager or general manager immediately after you have inspected the room. In these cases (especially if you have paid a premium over the standard rate to secure a better location or view), you should be able to negotiate a different room or a reduction in your room rate. If you fail to raise the question immediately upon checking into the room, your chances of recovering anything diminish greatly.

On the other hand, if your complaint is with the location of the hotel itself, rather than your individual room within the hotel, your options are limited once you have arrived at the property. Your best bet would be negotiating a refund with the hotel manager so that you may move to another hotel in the area.

Complaints about the physical appearance or condition of your room raise difficult questions, because one person's idea of *deluxe* or spacious may not agree with the hotel manager's notions. If you have concerns about your room, start by writing down your concerns. Be as specific and precise as you can. Complaints that revolve around commonly used hotel industry descriptions such as *two double beds* or *four-room suite* are the easiest to press. It is also a help if you have copies of any hotel brochures or materials that support your mental picture of what was promised to you, but not delivered.

Again, your very best recourse in these situations is negotiating a friendly compromise with the front desk manager or general manager. If you elect later to go to court with your dispute, your possible recovery will likely be very small (unless the hotel has engaged in a wholesale pattern of deception involving many other customers).

When judging a hotel's quality based on the number of *stars* or *diamonds* it has earned, remember that the United States has no standardized national system of rating hotels. However, in Europe and other parts of the world, national organizations actually govern the rating process based on hotels' service levels and luxury amenities. Marks awarded by AAA, Mobil, and other U.S. organizations are helpful to a degree, but they should not be considered absolute marks of quality. If a hotel claims a very high rating, ask which organization awarded the rating and take any unsubstantiated stars or diamonds with a grain of salt.

If you believe that your room is literally unsanitary, report the situation to the front desk and the housekeeping department immediately. If the hotel cannot clean the room to your satisfaction, ask firmly to be assigned a new room or given a refund. If your concerns go unheeded, you should contact local officials for a copy of the city and state health and safety codes that apply to hotels. In many cases, the hotel may actually be violating its own corporate rules or employee handbook regulations if a room is not sanitary. As a final resort, report unsafe conditions to local health authorities, as well as take photographs of the room in question for your records. (A $6 disposable camera may be a wise investment to document the problem.)

If you requested a nonsmoking room, keep in mind that hotels rarely guarantee that you will receive a nonsmoking room when you check in. Hotels set aside a certain number of rooms for nonsmokers. It is always possible that no nonsmoking rooms may be available when you arrive. If you feel that you were absolutely guaranteed a nonsmoking room upon arrival, talk to the front desk manager about a discount or other form of compensation for the inconvenience. If you have a medical condition, such as asthma, that requires you to stay in a nonsmoking room, and no such rooms are available (even though you requested this type of room when you made the reservation), the hotel should move you to a nonsmoking room in a different property and cover any difference in rates that you must pay.

Note: *Most states allow hotels to charge you an additional fee if you smoke in a nonsmoking room.*

Hotels are in constant renovation or general maintenance. As a result, you may have to live with the inconvenience of repairs going on around you. However, you have the right to ask for a room discount or other compensation in return or to move to another available room away from the construction.

INJURIES SUSTAINED AT HOTELS

Keeping guests safe and secure is one of the most critical obligations for any hotel. Many years ago, hotels were held to a *strict liability* standard—making the hotel responsible for any injury suffered by a guest, regardless of whether the hotel knew about the risks or potential hazards. Today, hotels still fall under a tough *duty of care* standard, requiring them to take all reasonable steps to protect you from harm resulting from the condition of their premises, other hotel guests, or even criminals.

Generally, hotels must warn you about known or potential hazards. This duty increases as the level of danger rises. For example, many properties post signs noting that building doors will be locked after a certain time each evening, after which guests must use their keys to gain access. However, they may not inform guests about a rash of car thefts in the neighborhood unless thefts have actually occurred on hotel premises. On the other hand, if the hotel gives you information that makes you act less cautiously than usual—such as telling you that it is safe to jog on streets surrounding the hotel—its owners could be held liable if you suffer injury or damages as a result.

If you fall on the hotel property due to slipping or tripping, the hotel may be liable for your injuries. Many slip-and-fall injuries occur as a result of common hazards, such as ice or snow on a sidewalk, spilled food or drink in the hotel bar or restaurant, or rainwater on the lobby floor. Other accidents happen due to building or design flaws, such as steep steps or stairs, poor parking lot lighting, or aging parts of the hotel in need of renovation.

In such cases, the hotel's duty of care begins not when the hazardous condition is created (for instance, when the snow falls on the sidewalk), but when the hotel fails to take reasonable steps to correct or remove the hazard. Simply slipping while on the hotel's premises does not constitute automatic liability—the key questions are whether the hotel knew about the problem and what it did to fix it.

The duty also begins when the hotel fails to comply with local building codes or neglects to take action to correct design flaws (such as installing nonskid surfaces on outside steps that are prone to freezing in winter conditions). If you suffer an injury that you believe is the result of building flaws, contact the local city government to ask questions about the building code, fire code, and health and safety ordinances that apply to the property. Hotels must follow a long list of state and local laws and regulations governing heating and cooling systems, water supply, electrical wiring and equipment, structural design, fire protection, and similar construction issues. If the hotel failed to follow the code properly, leading to your injury or damage, that failure may be judged *negligence per se*. In other words, the hotel cannot claim that its failure to act was reasonable, because laws are presumed on their face to be reasonable.

Also, the hotel must abide by the rules and procedures outlined in its employee, franchiser, and corporate manuals, as well as generally accepted lodging industry standards. For example, if the hotel's franchiser or parent company issues guidelines requiring its properties to provide motion-sensitive lights in its parking lots, but your hotel did not follow the guidelines and you suffered injury as a result, then this failure to abide by the franchiser's standards will likely constitute negligence.

With several high-profile blazes in the 1990s, fire safety has become a growing concern for hotels. Building code requirements to prevent or contain fires in hotels tend to be very stringent, because guests are usually not familiar with the property and may become confused in the event of an actual fire. If you are injured during a fire, any violation of the fire code could be grounds for holding the hotel liable. Examples include smoke detectors that do not work, a lack of emergency lighting or alarm systems, or confusing evacuation instructions posted for guests. This standard applies even if the hotel was not directly responsible for the fire, or if your injuries resulted from the evacuation itself rather than the actual blaze.

Swimming pools are another common cause of hotel injuries. While more claims arise as a result of bathroom slips and falls, larger jury awards result from swimming pool mishaps. Because pools constitute a larger obvious hazard to guests, hotels have a major responsibility to insure safety while installing, maintaining, and controlling access to pools. In many jurisdictions, basic steps such as posted *Swim At Your Own Risk* signs will not insulate the hotel from liability if it failed to take additional necessary steps to reduce potential dangers. Hotels have lost cases because courts decided that they must expect children, disabled travelers, and even guests who have been drinking too much to wander into the pool area and suffer harm.

Hotels have a duty to insure that the materials and furnishings used in their rooms are reasonably safe for everyday use. Generally, the hotel is considered to be in a better position to recognize and remedy such hazards and to secure insurance to cover related claims, so that you as the guest will not be forced to inspect every bed and desk chair in the entire hotel before using them.

In some cases, the hotel might be held liable for injuries even if it could not have directly prevented them. For example, a guest may sue the hotel for injuries sustained while eating breakfast in a restaurant on the hotel premises. Although the restaurant is owned and operated by an independent company, the hotel may be considered liable because the restaurant is situated on hotel property. The hotel owes its highest duty of care to paying guests.

While the courts have historically proved sympathetic to guests' claims against hotels, you do not have an unlimited right to recover damages if you are hurt because you acted without thinking or you ignored basic common sense. For example, if you decide to stand on a desk chair in your room at a bed-and-breakfast inn to adjust the ceiling fan over your bed, and the chair collapses under you, a judge might conclude that the inn is 80% liable for the shoddy state of the chair, but that you are 20% liable for using poor judgment in climbing atop the chair in the first place. Therefore, your $100,000 judgment is reduced to $80,000.

Crimes

If you are hurt as a result of crimes committed on or near hotel property, you may find it difficult to hold the hotel liable unless the crime could have been anticipated and prevented (for example, providing better lighting in the hotel parking lot). One exception to this rule is if the hotel is located in an area known to have a high crime rate. If that is the case, the hotel's general duty to warn you about hazardous conditions may require it to warn you about the possibility of crime in and around hotel property.

Whatever the crime rate may be, some courts may find the hotel at least partially liable for crimes if the hotel failed to take basic security steps such as installing working locks on guest room windows and doors. In one very famous case, the singer Connie Francis won a $2.5 million judgment against a hotel after she was physically assaulted in her hotel room; the court ruled that

Travel Tip

Follow these safety tips from hotel security experts.

- Upon checking in, make sure that no strangers hear your name and room number.

- Always use the hotel's main entrance.

- Check the windows and doors in your room for working locks.

- Never leave your room door open when carrying luggage or using vending machines.

the hotel was liable because her room's door locks could be easily opened from the outside.

If a hotel employee robs or injures you, generally, the hotel is responsible for all acts by its employees that are carried out within the scopes of their employment. Even if the worker commits a crime on hotel property while off duty or acting outside the scope of his or her employment, the hotel may be held liable because it owes guests the duty of care. Additionally, the hotel may be liable if it fails to supervise employees properly, or if it does not conduct a complete background check on the employee in question.

If another guest assaults you, a different standard applies. The hotel would be considered responsible only if the assault could have been foreseen and prevented. For example, the hotel should act if a guest is obviously drunk and becomes aggressive toward other guests in the corridor outside his or her room.

Stolen Property

Hotels have a special duty to receive and protect your personal belongings, as well as yourself. However, the duty for belongings can be limited reasonably by hotels. For example, the hotel will generally be allowed to prohibit firearms, hazardous substances, animals, and other personal property that could cause harm or concern for other guests or the hotel premises.

Many years ago, hotels were completely liable for any damage, loss, or theft of a guest's personal property. Today, however, most states have placed limits on a hotel's liability as long as it follows certain regulations. For example, hotels must provide a safe for storing a guest's cash, jewelry, and other valuable property. The hotel must inform guests that the safe is available for their use; that the hotel has limited liability for any items left in the safe; and, that the hotel may not be responsible if the guest chooses not to keep valuables in the safe.

Sometimes, hotels attempt to disclaim their liability completely with posted notices, such as *Management is not responsible for any loss suffered by guests or their belongings.* In these situations, the hotel is attempting to gain more protection than is allowed generally under state laws. As a result, the hotel may lose any liability protection offered and be held liable for the full amount of the guest's loss or injury.

The rules in many states give hotels leeway to accept valuables above a specified dollar amount. Many hotels today will provide notices (in the check-in materials or on notices posted in the rooms) limiting its liability to a certain dollar amount for items stored in the safe, unless the guest specifically declares a higher value. Some states have held that, when a hotel accepts items from a guest who has declared a stated value exceeding the statutory limit for hotel liability, then the hotel has waived its protection and must reimburse the guest for the full value if the goods are lost or destroyed. Other states limit the exposure to the statutory amount, even if the guest declared a higher value. Also, the liability limit should be conspicuously posted for you to read or the hotel may not be protected by the limit.

These statutory limits may not apply at all if the valuables were lost or destroyed due to the hotel's intentional or negligent acts. Many state laws limiting hotel liability were written to protect hotels from acts outside their control, such as tornadoes, fire, or armed robbery. If the hotel fails to use reasonable care in safeguarding guests' deposited property, such as routinely leaving the safe unlocked at night, then the hotel will likely be held completely liable for the full value of the property. Also, guests may recover against a hotel if it did not follow the letter of the state law limiting its liability. For example, if hotels are required to post conspicuous notices in guest rooms, but the hotel instead puts its notices on a piece of paper inside nightstand drawers, then guests may not have received adequate notice.

If you plan to stay in hotels while traveling with a large amount of cash, jewelry, or other valuables, find out ahead of time what the hotel's maximum liability in its state will be. Also, check your business liability, homeowners, and travel insurance policies to see if there are loopholes in your coverage that would prevent you from recovering the full value of your possessions (for example, a disclaimer saying you cannot file a claim if you failed to use the hotel's safe for storing the valuables).

You may travel with valuable property that cannot be easily stored in a hotel safe, but exceed statutory limits for hotel liability, such as designer dresses and fur coats. If these goods are lost or damaged, you may still be able to recover from the hotel if you can demonstrate its negligence. Some jurisdictions hold the hotel responsible only if it were *grossly* negligent. The line between simple negligence and gross negligence can be fine.

Centuries ago, hotels were strictly liable for protecting your horses, carriages, and other means of transportation. Today, hotels are required only to exercise reasonable care to protect your vehicles. In fact, many hotels post signs in its parking lots and print disclaimers on parking tickets expressly disclaiming any liability for guests' vehicles.

The situation changes, however, when it comes to guests' goods that are left in the care of the hotel, such as clothing given to the front desk clerk for the hotel's laundry service and luggage stored with the bellman in return for a claim check. This personal property falls under the theory of *bailment*, in which you (as the owner or *bailor*) leave goods in the care of another person (the *bailee*), who must return the goods to you at some future date or become liable for the full value of the goods. In the case of laundry, checked bags, and other guest property left in the hotel's custody, the hotel must exercise reasonable care in handling the goods or reimburse the guest for the full value if the goods are lost or damaged.

Seized Property

In extreme cases where a guest fails to pay the hotel charges, the hotel may choose to seize the guest's property (in the room, at the front desk, or at the bell stand) and sell it to cover the outstanding bill. Some states require the hotel to give the guest notice before selling the property, while others mandate sales at public auction with any cash raised in excess of the hotel bill returned to the guest. If the guest manages to pay the debt before the sale takes place, the property must be returned to the guest once the payment is made. Hotels can confiscate and sell a guest's property only to pay for a current hotel bill—if the guest owes money on a previous bill, the hotel cannot use these funds to satisfy that debt.

HOTEL SPECIFICS

ACCOR HOTELS
5300 North High Street
Columbus, OH   43214
800-221-4542
www.accorhotels.com

ADAM'S MARK HOTELS & RESORTS
11330 Olive Blvd.
St. Louis, MO   63141
800-444-2326
www.adamsmark.com

AMERISUITES
700 Route 46, East
Fairfield, NJ   07007
877-774-6467
www.amerisuites.com

ASTON HOTELS & RESORTS
2155 Kalakaua Avenue
Suite 500
Honolulu, HI   96815
877-997-6667
www.astonhotels.com

BARCELO HOTELS & RESORTS
Punta Cana
P.O. Box 3177
Higuey, Dominican Republic
800-924-5044
www.barcelo.com

BAYMONT INNS & SUITES
P.O. Box 2636
San Antonio, TX   78299
866-999-1111
www.baymontinns.com

BEST WESTERN INTERNATIONAL
P.O. Box 42007
Phoenix, AZ   85080-2007
800-780-7234
www.bestwestern.com

CAMBERLEY HOTELS
3060 Peachtree Road
Suite 1700
Atlanta, GA   30305
800-359-6552
www.camberleyhotels.com

CHOICE HOTELS INTERNATIONAL
10750 Columbia Pike
Silver Spring, MD   20901
877-424-6423
www.choicehotels.com

CLARION HOTELS, INNS, RESORTS & SUITES
10750 Columbia Pike
Silver Spring, MD   20901
877-424-6423
www.clarioninn.com

CLUB MED
75 Valencia Avenue
12th Floor
Coral Gables, FL   33134
888-932-2582
www.clubmed.com

COMFORT INNS & SUITES
10750 Columbia Pike
Silver Spring, MD   20901
877-424-6423
www.comfortinn.com

COUNTRY INNS & SUITES BY CARLSON
11340 Blondo Street
Omaha, NE   68164
800-456-4000
www.countryinns.com

COURTYARD BY MARRIOTT
Marriott Drive
Washington, D.C.   20058
888-236-2427
www.courtyard.com

CROWNE PLAZA HOTELS & RESORTS
3 Ravinia Drive
Suite 2900
Atlanta, GA   30346
800-2-CROWNE
www.crowneplaza.com

DAYS INNS OF AMERICA
1 Sylvan Way
Parsippany, NJ   07054
800-DAYS-INN
www.daysinn.com

DOUBLETREE HOTELS & RESORTS
9336 Civic Center Drive
Beverly Hills, CA   90210
800-222-8733
www.doubletree.com

DRURY HOTELS
10801 Pear Tree Lane
St. Louis, MO   63074
800-DRURY-INN
www.druryhotels.com

ECONO LODGE
10750 Columbia Pike
Silver Spring, MD   20901
877-424-6423
www.econolodge.com

EMBASSY SUITES HOTELS
9336 Civic Center Drive
Beverly Hills, CA 90210
800-EMBASSY
www.embassysuites.com

EXTENDED STAY AMERICA
100 Dunbar Street
Spartanburg, SC 29306
800-804-3724
www.extendedstayamerica.com

FAIRFIELD INN & SUITES BY MARRIOTT
Marriott Drive
Washington, DC 20058
800-228-2800
www.fairfieldinn.com

FAIRMONT HOTELS & RESORTS
100 Wellington Street West
P.O. Box 40
Toronto, ON M5K 1B7
CANADA
800-257-7544
www.fairmont.com

FOUR SEASONS HOTELS & RESORTS
1165 Leslie Street
Toronto, ON M3C 2K8
CANADA
800-819-5053
www.fourseasons.com

HAMPTON INNS & SUITES
9336 Civic Center Drive
Beverly Hills, CA   90210
800-426-7866
www.hamptoninn.com

HARRAH'S HOTELS
1 Harrah's Court
Las Vegas, NV 89119
800-HARRAHS
www.harrahs.com

HAWTHORN SUITES
13 Corporate Square
Suite 250
Atlanta, GA   30329
800-527-1133
www.hawthorn.com

HELMSLEY HOTELS
230 Park Avenue
New York, NY   10169
800-221-4982
www.helmsleyhotels.com

HILTON HOTELS
9336 Civic Center Drive
Beverly Hills, CA   90210
800-HILTONS
www.hilton.com

HILTON GARDEN INNS
9336 Civic Center Drive
Beverly Hills, CA   90210
877-STAY-HGI
www.hiltongardeninn.com

HISTORIC HOTELS OF AMERICA
1785 Massachusetts Ave. N.W.
Washington, DC   20036
202-588-6000
www.nationaltrust.org

HOLIDAY INN
3 Ravinia Drive
Suite 2900
Atlanta, GA   30346
800-HOLIDAY
www.holiday-inn.com

HOLIDAY INN EXPRESS
3 Ravinia Drive
Suite 2900
Atlanta, GA   30346
800-HOLIDAY
www.hiexpress.com

HOMEWOOD SUITES BY HILTON
9336 Civic Center Drive
Beverly Hills, CA   90210
800-225-5466
www.homewood-suites.com

HOWARD JOHNSON INTERNATIONAL
1 Sylvan Way
Parsippany, NJ   07054
800-446-4656
www.hojo.com

HYATT HOTELS & RESORTS
200 W. Madison Street
38th Floor
Chicago, IL   60606
800-233-1234
www.hyatt.com

INNS OF AMERICA
755 Raintree Drive
Suite 200
Carlsbad, CA   92009
800-826-0778
www.innsofamerica.com

INTERCONTINENTAL HOTELS & RESORTS
3 Ravinia Drive
Suite 2900
Atlanta, GA   30346
800-327-0200
www.interconti.com

JOIE DE VIVRE HOSPITALITY
567 Sutter Street
San Francisco, CA   94102
800-738-7477
www.jdvhospitality.com

JOLLY HOTELS
22 E. 38th Street
New York, NY   10016
800-221-2626
www.jollyhotels.it

KEMPINSKI HOTELS & RESORTS
99 Park Avenue
10th Floor
New York, NY   10016
800-426-3135
www.kempinski.com

KNIGHTS INN
1 Sylvan Way
Parsippany, NJ   07054
800-843-5644
www.knightsinn.com

LA QUINTA INNS & SUITES
P.O. Box 2636
San Antonio, TX   78299
800-725-1661
www.laquinta.com

LEADING HOTELS OF THE WORLD
99 Park Avenue
New York, NY   10016
800-745-8883
www.lhw.com

LE MERIDIEN HOTELS & RESORTS
420 Lexington Avenue
Suite 1718
New York, NY   10170
800-253-0861
www.lemeridien.com

LOEWS HOTELS
667 Madison Avenue
New York, NY   10021
800-23-LOEWS
www.loewshotels.com

MAINSTAY SUITES
10750 Columbia Pike
Silver Spring, MD   20901
877-424-6423
www.mainstaysuites.com

MANDARIN ORIENTAL HOTEL GROUP
509 Madison Avenue
Suite 1800
New York, NY   10022
866-526-6567
www.mandarin-oriental.com

MARC RESORTS HAWAII
2155 Kalakaua Avenue
3rd Floor
Honolulu, HI   96815
800-535-0085
www.marcresorts.com

MARRIOTT HOTELS, RESORTS & SUITES
Marriott Drive
Washington, DC   20058
800-228-9290
www.marriott.com

MOTEL 6
14651 Dallas Parkway
Suite 500
Dallas, TX   75254
800-4-MOTEL6
www.motel6.com

NEW OTANI HOTELS
520 Madison Avenue
24th Floor
New York, NY   10022
800-421-8795
www.newotanihotels.com

NIKKO HOTELS INTERNATIONAL
222 Mason Street
San Francisco, CA   94102
800-645-5687
www.nikkohotels.com

NOVOTEL
5300 N. High Street
Columbus, OH   43214
800-NOVOTEL
www.novotel.com

OBEROI HOTELS & RESORTS
509 Madison Avenue
Suite 1906
New York, NY   10022
800-5-OBEROI
www.oberoihotels.com

OMNI HOTELS
420 Decker Drive
Suite 200
Irving, TX   75062
800-THE-OMNI
www.omnihotels.com

OUTRIGGER HOTELS & RESORTS
2375 Kuhio Avenue
Honolulu, HI   96815-2992
800-688-7444
www.outrigger.com

PAN PACIFIC HOTELS & RESORTS
500 Post Street
San Francisco, CA   94102
800-327-8585
www.panpacific.com

PARK INN & PARK PLACE HOTELS
11340 Bondo Street
Omaha, NE   68164
800-670-7275
www.parkhtls.com

PREFERRED HOTELS & RESORTS WORLDWIDE
311 S. Wacker Drive
Suite 1900
Chicago, IL 60606
800-323-7500
www.preferredhotels.com

QUALITY INNS, HOTELS & SUITES
10750 Columbia Pike
Silver Spring, MD 20901
877-424-6423
www.qualityinn.com

RADISSON HOTELS & RESORTS WORLDWIDE
P.O. Box 59159
Minneapolis, MN 55459-8204
800-333-3333
www.radisson.com

RAMADA FRANCHISE SYSTEMS
1 Sylvan Way
Parsippany, NJ 07054
800-272-6232
www.ramada.com

RED LION HOTELS & INNS
201 W. North River Drive
Spokane, WA 99201
800-RED-LION
www.redlion.com

RED ROOF INNS
14651 Dallas Parkway
Suite 500
Dallas, TX 75254
800-RED-ROOF
www.redroof.com

REGAL HOTELS INTERNATIONAL
18/F Paliburg Plaza
68 Yee Wo Street
Causeway Bay, Hong Kong
800-222-8888
www.regalhotel.com

REGENT INTERNATIONAL HOTELS
P.O. Box 59159
Minneapolis, MN 55459-8254
800-545-4000
www.regenthotels.com

RELAIS & CHATEAUX
148 East 63rd Street
New York, NY 10021
800-RELAIS-8
www.relaischateaux.com

RENAISSANCE HOTELS & RESORTS
Marriott Drive
Washington, DC 20058
800-HOTELS-1
www.renaissancehotels.com

RESIDENCE INN BY MARRIOTT
Marriott Drive
Washington, DC   20058
800-331-3131
www.residenceinn.com

RITZ CARLTON HOTEL COMPANY
4445 Willard Avenue
Suite 800
Chevy Chase, MD   20815
800-241-3333
www.ritzcarlton.com

RODEWAY INNS
10750 Columbia Pike
Silver Spring, MD   20901
877-424-6423
www.rodewayinn.com

ROSEWOOD HOTELS & RESORTS
500 Crescent Court
Suite 300
Dallas, TX   75201
888-ROSEWOOD
www.rosewoodhotels.com

SANDALS RESORTS
4950 SW 72nd Avenue
Miami, FL   33155
800-SANDALS
www.sandals.com

SANDS RESORTS
P.O. Box 2998
Myrtle Beach, SC   29578
800-845-6701
www.sandsresorts.com

SHANGRI-LA HOTELS & RESORTS
5777 W. Century Boulevard
Suite 1105
Los Angeles, CA   90045
800-942-5050
www.shangri-la.com

SHERATON HOTELS & RESORTS
777 Westchester Avenue
White Plains, NY   10604
800-325-3535
www.sheraton.com

SHILO INNS & RESORTS
11600 SW Shilo Lane
Portland, OR   97225
800-222-2244
www.shiloinns.com

SHONEY'S INNS
130 Maple Drive North
Hendersonville, TN   37075
800-552-INNS
www.shoneysinn.com

SIGNATURE INN HOTELS
8 Perimeter Center East
Suite 8050
Atlanta, GA 30346
800-JAMESON
www.jamesoninns.com

SLEEP INNS
10750 Columbia Pike
Silver Spring, MD 20901
877-424-6423
www.sleepinn.com

SMALL LUXURY HOTELS OF THE WORLD
14673 Midway Road
Suite 201
Addison, TX 75001
800-525-4800
www.slh.com

SOFITEL
5300 N. High Street
Columbus, OH 43214
800-SOFITEL
www.sofitel.com

SOL MELIA HOTELS & RESORTS
1000 Brickell Avenue
Suite 500
Miami, FL 33131
888-95MELIA
www.solmelia.com

SONESTA INTERNATIONAL HOTELS
116 Huntington Avenue
Boston, MA 02116
800-SONESTA
www.sonesta.com

STARWOOD HOTELS & RESORTS WORLDWIDE
1111 Westchester Avenue
White Plains, NY 10604
914-640-8100
www.starwood.com

STAYBRIDGE SUITES BY HOLIDAY INN
3 Ravinia Drive
Suite 2900
Atlanta, GA 30346
800-238-8000
www.staybridgesuites.com

STERLING HOTELS & RESORTS
311 S. Wacker Drive
Suite 1900
Chicago, IL 60606
800-637-7200
www.sterlinghotels.com

ST. REGIS HOTELS
777 Westchester Avenue
White Plains, NY 10604
888-625-5144
www.stregis.com

STUDIOPLUS HOTELS

100 Dunbar Street
Suite 200
Spartanburg, SC 29306
800-804-3724
www.extendedstayamerica.com

SUMMIT HOTELS & RESORTS

200 W. 57th Street
Suite 502
New York, NY 10019
800-457-4000
www.summithotels.com

SUPER 8 MOTELS

1910 8th Ave., NE
P.O. Box 4090
Aberdeen, SD 57402-4090
800-800-8000
www.super8.com

SUPERCLUBS

2021 Hayes Street
P.O. Box 222800
Hollywood, FL 33020
800-GO-SUPER
www.superclubs.com

TAJ HOTELS, RESORTS & PALACES

99 Park Avenue
New York, NY 10016
800-44-UTELL
www.tajhotels.com

THISTLE HOTELS
1800 E. Lambert Road
Suite 220
Brea, CA 92821
800-847-4358
www.thistlehotels.com

TRAVELODGE/THRIFTLODGE HOTELS
1 Sylvan Way
Parsippany, NJ 07054
800-578-7878
www.travelodge.com

VAGABOND INNS
5933 W. Century Boulevard
Suite 200
Los Angeles, CA 90045-5461
800-522-1555
www.vagabondinn.com

VILLAGER FRANCHISE SYSTEMS
1 Sylvan Way
Parsippany, NJ 07054
800-843-5644
www.villager.com

WARWICK INTERNATIONAL HOTELS
65 W. 54th Street
New York, NY 10019
800-203-3232
www.warwickhotels.com

WELLESLEY INNS & SUITES
700 Route 46 East
Fairfield, NJ   07004
800-444-8888
www.wellesleyonline.com

WESTIN HOTELS & RESORTS
777 Westchester Avenue
White Plains, NY   10604
800-WESTIN-1
www.westin.com

WESTMARK HOTELS
221 First Avenue West
Suite 100
Seattle, WA   98119
800-544-0970
www.westmarkhotels.com

W HOTELS
777 Westchester Avenue
White Plains, NY   10604
877-946-8357
www.whotels.com

WINGATE INNS
1 Sylvan Way
Parsippany, NJ   07054
800-228-1000
www.wingateinns.com

WYNDHAM HOTELS & RESORTS
1950 Stemmons Freeway
Suite 6001
Dallas, TX 75207
800-WYNDHAM
www.wyndham.com

chapter four:
Cruises

From the white glove service days of the *Titanic* to the star-studded days aboard the *Love Boat*, ocean cruises have continued growing as an extremely popular vacation option. But *cruise* means more than just a bed on the ship and passage from one port to another. Along with accommodations and transportation (including, at times, airline tickets and airport transfers), the typical cruise package is comprised of meals, entertainment, shopping, gaming, shore tours, spa visits, and the latest twists—such as ice-skating rinks and rock-climbing walls.

MAKING YOUR CRUISE RESERVATION

Travel agencies book nineteen of every twenty cruises purchased in the United States. Some cruise lines do accept *direct bookings* from consumers via their toll-free reservation numbers and their websites, but you will rarely receive any discounts or extra benefits for doing so. However, regardless of how you book it, before you finalize your cruise booking, follow these initial steps.

- Ask your travel agent for candid advice about the cruise line's *word of mouth* reputation for customer service, as well as any horror stories from the agent's other clients about the specific ship you have chosen or about the company's ability to handle refunds and cancellations. Check out leading cruise ship guide-books for their reviews. National magazines such as *Conde Nast Traveler* routinely rank cruise lines for customer satisfaction.

- While they may be shocked at your request (because so few consumers take the time to read them), reputable cruise lines will gladly send you a copy of their current cruise ticket terms so that you can read the fine print at your leisure. Many lines post the terms on their websites or you may check **www.mytravelrights.com** for the latest versions, as well.

Literally, the cruise ticket is your contract for the trip. As you read the terms, look specifically for the rules governing disputes to determine the requirements for filing a claim with, or bringing a lawsuit against, the cruise line.

- Find out about available price breaks based on the travel season or on your ability to book a required number of months in advance of your sailing. Request a guarantee from the cruise line that you will be protected if it decides to lower its rates closer to departure. Many cruise companies engage in last-minute discounting to fill empty cabins closer to its sailing dates, but not every cruise line will match that rate for you if you have already placed a deposit on the same cruise at a higher price.

Know Before You Go

For many cruise lines, January is Wave Month—the busiest time of the year for bookings. Ask your travel agent to compare Wave Month deals to any savings you might get by booking closer to the sailing date.

- Given the extensive publicity generated by outbreaks of gastrointestinal illnesses aboard several ships, find out how your ship fared on its most recent sanitation inspection by the U.S. Public Health Service. (See p.121 for more on ship sanitation.)

- In the past, several major cruise lines were sued for deceptive advertising practices when they padded their basic fares by lumping in port charges, fuel fees, and other expenses without itemizing them for consumers to review. Now, all reputable lines voluntarily itemize port charges, taxes, and other fees that are not part of the actual base cruise charges.

Know Before You Go

Surprised when you boarded the ship for your *all inclusive vacation*—and were hit immediately with charges for soft drinks, ice cream, and even onboard restaurant reservations? Many ships now add fees for some services. Ask your travel agent or the cruise line for a list of what is not included in the basic cruise price.

- If you have a chronic medical condition, check ahead to inquire whether the ship has a doctor on board at all times who speaks English. You have the right to ask about the doctor's qualifications and experience, too.

  Before you leave, remember to make and take with you copies of your prescriptions and (if you have a chronic condition) your most recent medical records.

- Generally speaking, you should always purchase *third-party travel insurance*—policies that are offered and administered by companies that are not owned by the cruise line itself. This is important if the cruise line declares bankruptcy or ceases operations, its travel insurance may not be in force to cover your damages.

Travel Tip

Some travel insurance companies no maintain a list of cruise lines for whic they will not issue coverage, based c concerns about the company's financi. stability or service record. If your cruis line appears on one of these lists, thir twice about sailing.

If you do opt to purchase insurance from the cruise line directly, check the terms of your policy very carefully. Many cruise line policies are not actually travel insurance, but rather *cancellation penalty waivers* or *cancellation protections* that give you the chance to cancel your cruise without paying the usual penalties for canceling. The value of these waivers is negligible, because many of them are only effective until a few days before your sailing date. Therefore, if you must cancel your trip at the last minute, or during the cruise itself, you are fully liable for the cost of the cruise. True trip cancellation/trip interruption insurance offered by third-party vendors will give you much more comprehensive coverage.

YOUR TICKET

As a cruise passenger, your rights depend largely upon two factors—the terms of the cruise ticket you purchased and the prevailing maritime law (the law of the sea) that applies to passengers aboard ships.

Your cruise ticket is a *contract of carriage*. Under this contract, the cruise line has agreed not only to provide seagoing transportation for you from your home port to the final destination port (or back to the home port), but also to offer the agreed-upon levels of room and board and to provide a safe, clean, dependable vessel for your travels. While you may not find these promises listed specifically in your ticket, they are considered implied terms in the contract and obligations that the cruise line cannot ignore.

When you inspect the actual ticket, you will see basic information, such as the sailing date, the total price, and the location of your cabin. The ticket also contains fine print giving the cruise line permission to change the cruise itinerary, skip ports, and limit its liabilities toward you. As with rental car agreements, cruise tickets are final offers, and it is not likely that you will succeed in negotiating any of the fine-print terms in your cruise ticket. The courts will likely enforce all of the cruise ticket provisions unless you can show that they are highly unfair or unreasonable.

You must be given adequate notice of the terms of your cruise ticket in order for them to be considered enforceable. In most cases, you will see a statement printed in your ticket that says other terms have been

Travel Tip

Many cruise ships now host business and association conferences onboard. If you attend a shipboard conference, make sure you check the rules for deducting part or all of the cruise expenses from your taxes. (See Chapter 8 for details.)

incorporated into the contract. Whether you have actually read and understood the terms does not matter. The cruise line must simply prove that it gave you the terms early enough that you had a clear opportunity to read them.

On the other hand, the courts have split on whether you have truly received adequate notice if you booked your cruise through a travel agency or travel club and your documents were not forwarded to you until a short time before departure. In one case, the passengers received their cruise tickets a few days before the sailing date, leaving them no time to protest the ticket terms without risking the cancellation of their trip and the loss of their cruise payments. The court held that they did not receive sufficient notice. However, the primary factor is whether you had a sufficient opportunity to read and review the cruise ticket terms, not whether you actually did so. You have a stronger case if any delays in receiving your cruise documents can be blamed on the cruise line rather than yourself.

MARITIME LAW

Unlike other types of travel rights disputes, U.S. federal or state law rarely governs complaints against cruise lines. Instead, they fall under the control of *maritime law*—the *code of the seas* built upon centuries of legal principles for ships and sailing as interpreted by courts throughout the entire world. Maritime law is an arcane area of jurisprudence that takes precedence over basic

U.S. consumer protection measures (though, strangely enough, you will typically file a lawsuit under maritime law in a U.S. federal or state courtroom).

What does this mean for you? Cruise line attorneys know every trick in the maritime law books, so you must have a firm grasp of your rights as a cruise passenger before you purchase your trip on the high seas (and, if you pursue a case against a cruise line, an attorney experienced in maritime law).

If your cruise begins or ends in a port located in another country besides the U.S., your cruise ticket may stipulate that the laws of that country govern your trip. It does not matter that you are an American citizen who purchased the cruise package in the United States. However, U.S. courts may take into consideration the cruise itinerary, the cruise line's nation of registry, the actual ticket terms you were given, and other factors before deciding whether you will be bound by the foreign laws.

If you chose a cruise that never touches the U.S.—that is, the entire itinerary begins and ends in foreign ports on a cruise line registered in another country—then you run the risk that U.S. courts will have no jurisdiction at all. You may be forced to file your claim in the cruise line's nation of registry, with limits on your damage claims set by the terms of the *Athens Convention* (an international maritime treaty that the United States has never ratified).

If you decide to sue a cruise line, be prepared for an uphill battle. Most cruise tickets require you to file a written claim describing your damaged or lost property, breach of contract, or similar complaints within ten days of the incident. You must file your lawsuit within six months. Personal injury claims must be filed with the cruise line within six months of the injury, with the lawsuit filed within one year.

It is absolutely critical that you hire an attorney experienced in maritime law cases, rather than a local personal injury attorney or your family lawyer. U.S. federal and state laws do not apply across the board to cruise line cases, and if you miss these filing deadlines by even a single day, you have lost your chance to pursue the claim. Cruise line attorneys have been known to suggest negotiating a settlement with a disgruntled passenger who then forgets to watch the deadlines for filing a formal claim. Feel free to talk to the cruise line representatives about settling, but keep an eye on your filing deadlines, too.

FILING SUIT

Your cruise ticket probably includes a *forum selection clause* requiring you to bring your legal action in one particular jurisdiction (typically, the cruise line's nation of registry). The clause may state that this location holds exclusive jurisdiction, meaning that you cannot file suit in any other court. Generally, U.S. courts have upheld forum selection clauses, even if they require American citizens to travel overseas in order to pursue the claim. In very limited instances, your attorney may succeed in arguing that the clause is unfair or unreasonable, but consider that most cruise lines have defended their forum selections in many previous cases.

Among every mode of travel, cruise lines pose the toughest challenge for travelers determined to protect their rights. In many instances, your very best strategy is complaining (politely, but very firmly) to the officers aboard the ship while the cruise is underway.

CANCELLED SAILINGS

If the cruise line cancels the entire sailing, you should qualify for a complete refund of your initial deposit and any additional payments you have made to date. After you have been notified about the cancellation, send a fax or letter to the cruise line (copied to your travel agent) demanding a full, immediate refund. Ask for not only your cruise deposit and additional payments, but also your other damages such as the loss of your nonrefundable airline tickets and any extra expenses you incurred specifically because the cruise line cancelled the sailing. Similar rules apply if the cruise line reschedules your sailing for

Travel Tip

Many cruise lines introduced cancel for any reason policies in 2003. If you book a cruise, you may change your mind (even the day before you sail) and request a cash refund or future cruise credit.

new dates that are not acceptable to you.

Increasingly, cruise lines will attempt to offer canceled passengers credits for a future cruise *in lieu* of a cash refund. If you strongly prefer cash, you must raise your objections immediately. While no laws specifically require a cash refund, the company may agree with you to keep you as a happy customer. (Another option is asking your credit card company for a charge back on your payments.)

Do not delay filing this written refund request with the cruise line, as cancelled cruises can be a sure sign that the company is in financial trouble. If the cruise line declares bankruptcy, your refund may be tied up in bankruptcy court for several years and you run the risk (after larger creditors are paid) that you will receive only pennies on the dollar.

All cruise lines that operate from any U.S. port or in U.S. waters must post a bond or other surety with the *Federal Maritime Commission* (FMC) to protect passenger funds in the event of nonperformance. The amount of the required bond varies depending on the cruise line's revenues. Currently, the maximum ceiling on the bond amount is $15 million. Because other creditors like food service vendors and fuel companies may also file claims against an FMC bond, passengers involved in recent cruise bankruptcies such as Regency Cruises and Premier Cruises have found themselves still fighting years later in bankruptcy court for a partial refund of their lost deposits or payments.

Therefore, though the cruise lines point to their FMC bonds as a protection for consumers, in practice the bond may not provide enough assets to pay back in full all of the disgruntled passengers who have lost money. By far, the safest course of action when making a cruise deposit or final payment is using a major credit card.

SKIPPED PORTS

Most cruises are planned around several scheduled port stops or *calls*, where the ship docks in or near a city so that cruise passengers can leave the ship and explore the destination for several hours or even a day or more. For many travelers, the port stops can be a major reason for choosing a particular cruise vacation. If the cruise does not make one or more port stops that were promised in the original itinerary, then in essence you will not receive the full value of what you paid for when you bought the trip.

Your cruise ticket will likely include a disclaimer giving the cruise line the right to cancel a scheduled port stop or to change the entire itinerary without advance notice. Beyond this disclaimer, general maritime law gives the ship's captain the right to change the scheduled itinerary as required due to issues such as treacherous weather or the outbreak of war.

Whether you may request compensation for itinerary changes is largely a question of the degree of the changes. Generally, if the schedule changes were so severe that they devalued the overall cruise experience, you may succeed in claiming damages despite the cruise ticket disclaimer. For example, one family sued successfully when the cruise ship skipped two ports on a Caribbean cruise, arrived very late at the third port, and anchored in the harbor (not the pier) at the fourth port so that passengers had to be ferried in small, uncomfortable tenders to and from the shore.

If you argue successfully for compensation based on itinerary changes, the cruise ticket disclaimer usually limits the line's liability to a prorated share of your cruise fare. For example, if your seven-day cruise is cut short to four days, you could be entitled to a refund of ³⁄₇ of the price you paid for the trip.

If the itinerary changes actually remove your primary motivation for taking a cruise in the first place, you may actually win a larger share of your cruise fare. For example, if your ten-day Greek Isles cruise in the Mediterranean were cut short to five days, resulting in the cancellation of all scheduled port calls in the Greek Islands, you could argue that you received much less than half of the expected value of the trip.

SWITCHING CABINS

Occasionally, the cruise line will assign you (before you have boarded the ship, or after the cruise has begun) a different cabin than you reserved. If your new cabin is a better choice in a higher category, then you actually benefit from the move.

However, if you have been switched to a smaller or less desirable cabin, then the cruise line should refund the difference in price between your original cabin and the one you have been given. If the new cabin is in the same price range and category as your original cabin, you will have a tougher argument unless the new location brings its own set of problems (for example, it sits next to a noisy engine room). In this case, you should let the ship's purser or your cabin steward know immediately that you are unhappy and that you wish to be reassigned to a better cabin or given a partial refund. (You should definitely complain about this situation while you are aboard the ship, instead of waiting until the cruise has ended, as you will have a stronger claim against the cruise line at that point.)

UNSATISFACTORY CABINS

Sometimes cruise passengers are surprised at the small size of ship cabins compared to standard hotel rooms. Unless your cabin is literally smaller in size than the dimensions promised in the cruise brochure, you have no reasonable grounds for complaining. However, if conditions inside the cabin are unsafe or uncomfortable (such as a broken window or air conditioning that does not work), you have the right to ask for immediate repairs or a switch to a different cabin.

Also, you must accept that any cruise comes with a certain level of noise and motion on board. However, you do have the right to *quiet enjoyment* of your cruise. So, if your cabin sits next to the ship's boiler room with clanking noises that keep you awake throughout the night, you should contact your room steward or the purser immediately for a cabin change.

SHIP SANITATION

Cruise lines must obey many health, safety, and sanitation laws and regulations, many of them enforced by the U.S. Coast Guard. Federal officials have the primary responsibility for monitoring compliance with these rules, to the point of filing lawsuits and assessing fines to enforce them. However, if you have suffered damages or injuries as a direct result of an alleged infraction of a health, safety, or sanitation regulation, then the courts may consider the rule breaking as a breach of your cruise contract.

For example, several cruise ships were removed from service in 2002 as a result of outbreaks of the *Norwalk* gastrointestinal virus that caused a form of stomach flu among passengers and crew members. Some passengers filed lawsuits against the cruise lines involved, alleging that the lines could have prevented the illnesses by observing required sanitation procedures on the ships.

Cruise ships that sail from U.S. ports undergo periodic inspections by the U.S. Public Health Service to grade their compliance with federal sanitation rules. On a 100-point scale, individual ships are judged on the overall cleanliness of the vessel, as well as the quality of their water and food. Scores of 86 and above are satisfactory, but the real test is posting a series of consistently high marks over a period of several years. You can find the latest score for your cruise ship in the U.S. Public Health Service's *Biweekly Summary of Sanitation Inspections of International Cruise Ships*. It is also available online at **www.cdc.gov/nceh/vsp**.

> ### Travel Tip
> Worried about future outbreaks of the *Norwalk* virus? Federal health officials insist that the risk of falling ill at sea have actually decreased steadily since 1990. Simply wash your hands often and report any illness immediately to the ship's doctor.

Travel Tip

If you believe a health or safety violation caused problems on the cruise, you can submit a request to the U.S. Coast Guard for copies of its most recent ship inspection reports for your vessel.

If you become sick during a cruise, and you believe that the food or water on board caused your illness, alert ship officials immediately and ask for compensation. If they do not agree, request the latest federal sanitation reports for the vessel. While this report may not specifically say that the ship's food or water was found to be contaminated during the most recent inspection, a pattern of low sanitation scores in general will give you ammunition for your claim.

If the cruise line will not provide you with a copy of the latest report, send your request upon your return home to:

Vessel Sanitation Program
National Center for Environmental Health
U.S. Centers for Disease Control and Prevention
4770 Buford Highway NE
Building 101, MS-F23
Atlanta, GA 30341
800-323-2132

Enclose a letter indicating the name of the cruise line, the name of the ship, the embarkation and disembarkation ports, and the sailing dates.

ON-BOARD ILLNESS OR INJURY

The cruise line has a general duty to provide you with safe, clean, and sanitary services and facilities. Therefore, you can submit damage claims for illnesses, injuries, or even death caused by the company's negligent or intentional acts.

Cruise lines become negligent when they fail to take reasonable care, under the circumstances, to protect you from harm.

The key factors in determining negligence include:

- the company had actual knowledge of the danger (or even *constructive knowledge*, meaning that the danger had existed long enough that the cruise line should have known about it and taken steps to remedy it);
- the danger was a significant risk to your health or safety; and,
- the danger is linked to ocean travel (not an ordinary run-of-the-mill risk that you might have easily encountered if you had stayed at home).

For instance, the cruise line may be primarily responsible if you burn yourself using the specially designed hot-water faucet in your cabin bathroom, but it may not be held at fault if you break an ankle attempting a figure-eight turn on the ice skating rink.

If you believe that the cruise line should be held responsible for your injury, you should file a claim to recover your medical expenses, lost earnings, pain and suffering, and compensation for any resulting disability. Your ability to recover damages depends greatly on the warnings of danger the cruise line gives. The cruise line must take *reasonable care*—meaning that the cruise line should warn you about any hazards that you might not readily notice. These warnings do not necessarily have to be given in writing, but they must be conspicuous enough that you will receive adequate notice that a danger exists. For instance, if you carry your lunch into a roped-off section of the poolside cafe and then slip on the wet deck and hit your head while leaving, then many courts would say the rope barrier constituted adequate notice of the danger and you should have exercised reasonable care.

Moreover, the cruise line should warn you about natural risks such as storms and choppy seas. It must take every reasonable step to ensure that passengers follow its safety instructions. Shortly after you board the ship, for example, you will take part in a mandatory lifeboat drill. Ship personnel will go to great lengths to document the fact that every single passenger showed up and took part in the drill. However, cruise lines do not have to warn you about accidents that it cannot foresee or prevent (such as tidal waves), nor does it have to take extraordinary steps such as bolting all poolside chairs to the deck.

Many cruise ship claims result from slip-and-fall injuries, where the passenger suffers a fall on wet flooring or stumbles over a sill (the low barriers used on many vessels to keep water from moving around decks). One primary question in establishing the cruise line's responsibility in these instances is whether, at the time of your injury, you were engaged in an activity that is directly related to cruising, as opposed to something you might have easily been doing on shore.

For example, if you strain your back because you slipped while walking for exercise around the ship's wet promenade deck, the cruise line would likely be liable only if it could have foreseen the reason for your slip and taken steps to prevent it. However, if you slipped in the ship's corridor during rough weather because the handrail was damaged or missing, then the cruise line is likely at fault because the company has more experience dealing with storms and should have replaced the rail.

Many such safety-related injuries tend to occur in cabins, especially entering and exiting bathrooms (given the sills on the floor for catching water runoff that are set higher than usual for many passengers) and getting in and out of the smaller beds common on many ships. If you believe that your cabin is unsafe, the best strategy is alerting your cabin steward immediately. Your claim will hinge on whether you should have obviously noticed the cause of the injury and, if so, whether you took any steps to notify the cruise line so that it could fix the problem.

It is the cruise line's responsibility to provide safe methods of boarding and departing the ship. The company may provide, for example, a ramp with sides or handrails that extends completely from the pier to the ship entrance. When the ship is anchored in ports that do not have ramp access, the cruise line must provide safe tenders or boats to transport you to shore.

If you are injured on or near the pier or dock, the fault may lie with the dock owner, the port authority, the cruise line, or other parties. If the injury occurs in a foreign port, you will find it extremely challenging to file a claim, especially if the dock is owned or operated by the government.

Because cruise lines are not generally required to have a doctor on board (although almost every ship serving U.S. markets does), ship doctors are generally independent contractors rather than cruise line employees. If you believe the ship doctor injured you, your malpractice claim must be lodged against the doctor individually, not the cruise line.

However, the company may be judged liable if it contracted with a doctor without a license or with a record of medical mishaps that the cruise line should have found by conducting routine background checks. Know that the doctor may be licensed by another government, however, and he or she does not have to be licensed to practice in the United States even if serving aboard a ship catering to U.S. travelers.

Medical evacuations from cruise ships are a common occurrence, with many of them taking place via helicopter. While the U.S. Coast Guard assists in some emergencies, it is not obligated to provide free medical evacuations for U.S. citizens. You should check the fine print in your travel and health insurance policies to determine if you are covered for medical evacuations. You may consider additional protection, such as buying a membership in an emergency medical transportation organization like *SkyMed International*. (See Chapter 8 for details.)

Crimes

Unfortunately, crimes aboard ship have become more common. If you are physically attacked during your cruise, the company's liability depends largely on its relationship to your assailant. If he or she is a fellow passenger, the cruise line may be responsible if it knew (or should have known) that the person posed a possible danger to others, such as a drunk passenger who becomes belligerent in one of the ship's public spaces.

If the attacker is a crew member, the cruise line is likely liable if it is judged negligent in its hiring or supervision of the employee.

Know Before You Go

A state can rarely prosecute a crime that occurs in international waters. However, the Supreme Court of Florida ruled recently that the state may prosecute cruise ship crimes, even if the vessel is beyond the state's territorial waters. The case involved an assault on a U.S. citizen 100 miles from Florida's coast, in which no government prosecuted the crime.

If the company took standard precautions in screening the crew member's background and in supervising him or her, and if other safety procedures are in place (such as working locks on all passenger cabin doors), then the cruise line may escape responsibility. However, other courts have held the company *absolutely liable* for the criminal actions of its crew members.

Terrorist Attacks

A pressing worry today is the possibility of a terrorist attack on a cruise ship. In the famous case of the *Achille Lauro*, the courts ruled that the cruise line was responsible for taking reasonable safety precautions to prevent an attack on its passengers. However, the courts also ruled that the company had no specific duty to search its passengers for weapons when they boarded the cruise. (Because cruise embarkation procedures after the September 11 tragedies now routinely include metal detector screenings, x-ray baggage machines, and even personal searches, some legal experts believe that cruise lines may absorb at least partial liability in the future if terrorists conduct a successful attack on a cruise ship.)

SERVICE COMPLAINTS

If your sole complaint is that you simply did not enjoy your cruise experience, you have no real grounds for a claim against the cruise line. If you can trace your concerns to specific onboard service or facility issues—for example, the world-class spa pictured in the cruise brochure was closed for the entire cruise or the Broadway entertainers promised in cruise brochures did not perform as advertised—then you may be able to press your claim successfully.

Your claim will be much stronger if you are complaining about a string of service or equipment problems that, taken together, led to your extreme disappointment with the cruise. Also, it matters whether these incidents were foreseeable or within the control of the cruise line. For instance, you will probably not prevail if you sue because it rained constantly during the trip or if another person at your assigned dinner table spilled red wine on your new formal gown.

Luxury, *first class*, and *ultra-luxury* cruises bear a different standard. On these voyages—which can cost you several hundred dollars or more per day—you are indeed paying for top-notch service levels and extremely comfortable accommodations. If the cruise line or its crew members fail to meet these standards, you can argue that the company breached its contract with you.

BAGGAGE

Because cruises typically offer onboard receptions and formal dress events as part of the schedule, many passengers pack their tuxedos and evening gowns, fine jewelry, digital cameras, and other valuable belongings. If your luggage is damaged, lost, or stolen on the way to or during the cruise, you could suffer higher losses than on the usual vacation.

When it comes to baggage handling, the biggest difference between cruise lines and other modes of travel (especially airlines) is that the lines rarely handle or stow your bags. For the majority of the cruise, your luggage will be kept inside your own cabin, under your direct control. The only exceptions will be the brief periods (several hours long) when you board the ship at the home port pier and when you leave the ship at the end of the cruise. At those times, cruise

Travel Tip

When you pack for your cruise, include extra items like batteries and film that you may need on board. You may regret paying the ship's inflated gift shop prices for these basic items.

line employees or agents typically transfer bags on and off the vessel. (Many cruise passengers do not realize that the porter who helps with luggage at the pier may be an independent porter or longshoreman who does not work for the cruise line. If the porter damages, loses, or steals your luggage, the cruise line bears no direct responsibility.)

Your cruise ticket usually contains language limiting the cruise line's liability when its employees are at fault for damaging, losing, or stealing your baggage. As long as you received adequate notice of these terms, the cruise line will likely escape any responsibility for your losses. What makes this a challenge for some passengers is that many cruise lines set these limits at unreasonably low levels—typically, a grand total of $100 for your luggage, including formal wear, jewelry, and the luggage itself. You should consider buying additional insurance to cover your possessions, or check your homeowners or renters insurance to determine whether the policy offers any protection while you are traveling with these belongings.

Portable valuables such as heirloom jewelry should be stored in the ship's safe while you are on board. During the embarkation process at the home port, tell a cruise line staffer that you want to declare officially the actual value of your possessions, so that your estimate is on record with the company if the worst happens.

You must observe closely the deadlines posted in your cruise ticket for filing a claim with the cruise line for damaged, lost, or stolen baggage. Some companies only allow a few days to notify them of your loss and a couple of months in which to file any legal action. The courts have not been sympathetic to passengers who failed to meet those requirements. In one famous case, a passenger claimed to have lost more than $60,000 in jewelry and other valuables after a cruise ship fire. However, she lost because she missed both the 10-day limit for filing her claim and the six-month deadline for filing a lawsuit (conditions that were spelled out clearly in the cruise ticket).

PRICE CHANGES

Because the cruise industry has expanded so aggressively in recent years, many companies now discount their fares until the last possible minute. Do not be surprised to find lower rates available for your sailing and your cabin category after you have already paid in full for your ticket. While this practice of multiple fares is not illegal, you can protect yourself by asking the cruise line for a written guarantee that you will receive a cash or credit refund if the same type of cabin on your sailing is offered for a lower fare after you purchase your ticket.

Sometimes, cruise lines will offer cabin category upgrades (better cabins on higher decks) to passengers who book early. Let your travel agent or the cruise line know if you would like to receive free upgrades; then, when the offer arrives, you can check fares to decide if you would prefer a refund of the difference in fares or the upgrade.

MISSED CONNECTIONS

If you booked your airline flight through the cruise line's *air/sea program*, then the cruise line should be completely responsible for any delays or cancellations that make you miss the departure of your ship. The company should fly you to the next port on the ship's itinerary at its cost and pay any hotel and meal expenses while you are waiting for the replacement flight. (Sometimes, cruise ships have even delayed their departure if a large group is delayed on a flight.) If the cruise line booked you on a flight with connections, you may prefer asking for a direct flight (called an *air deviation*) for an additional $35-$75 fee.

If you booked the flight on your own, then the cruise line has no responsibility to rebook your flight or assist you with expenses. However, you should contact the cruise line immediately if your flight is delayed or canceled so that the ship knows about the problem. Also, you should consider travel insurance that covers trip delays.

DISABLED PASSENGERS

Generally speaking, most cruise ships operating in U.S. ports are flagged (registered) in other nations; therefore, they claim that they are exempted from the accessibility requirements of the *Americans with Disabilities Act*. However, the U.S. Supreme Court agreed in late 2004 to review a case brought by disabled passengers against Norwegian Cruise Line (NCL) because they were forced to pay higher fares to use accessible cabins aboard NCL's ships. Observers predict a final decision from the court by June 2005.

If you have a disability that may affect your enjoyment of a cruise vacation, alert your travel agent or the cruise line at the time of booking to determine whether the line has accessible cabins and public areas that will make your cruise more comfortable.

CRUISE LINE SPECIFICS

AMERICAN CRUISE LINES
741 Boston Post Road
Suite 200
Guilford, CT   06437
800-814-6880
www.americancruiselines.com

AMERICAN WEST STEAMBOAT COMPANY
2101 Fourth Avenue
Suite 1150
Seattle, WA   98121
800-434-1232
www.americanweststeamboat.com

CARNIVAL CRUISE LINES
3655 NW 87th Avenue
Miami, FL   33178
800-438-6744
www.carnival.com

CELEBRITY CRUISES
1050 Caribbean Way
Miami, FL   33132
800-437-3111
www.celebritycruises.com

CIRCLE LINE
Pier 83
W. 42nd Street & Hudson River
New York, NY 10036
212-630-8885
www.circleline42.com

CLIPPER CRUISE LINE
11969 Westline Industrial Drive
St. Louis, MO 63146
800-325-0010
www.clippercruise.com

COSTA CRUISES
200 South Park Road
Suite 200
Hollywood, FL 33021-8541
800-33-COSTA
www.costacruises.com

CRUISE WEST
2301 Fifth Avenue
Suite 401
Seattle, WA 98121
888-851-8133
www.cruisewest.com

CRYSTAL CRUISES
2049 Century Park East
Suite 1400
Los Angeles, CA 90067
310-785-9300
www.crystalcruises.com

CUNARD LINE
6100 Blue Lagoon Drive
Suite 400
Miami, FL 33126
800-7-CUNARD
www.cunard.com

DELTA QUEEN STEAMBOAT COMPANY
1380 Port of New Orleans Place
New Orleans, LA 70130
800-543-1949
www.deltaqueen.com

DISCOVERY CRUISE LINE
1775 NW 70th Avenue
Miami, FL 33126
800-866-8687
www.discoverycruiseline.com

DISNEY CRUISE LINE
P.O. Box 10238
Lake Buena Vista, FL 32830-0210
800-511-1333
www.disneycruise.com

FIRST EUROPEAN CRUISES
95 Madison Avenue
Suite 609
New York, NY 10016
206-281-3535
www.first-european.com

HOLLAND AMERICA LINE
300 Elliott Avenue West
Seattle, WA 98119
206-281-3535
www.hollandamerica.com

MEDITERRANEAN SHIPPING CRUISES (USA)
420 Fifth Avenue
New York, NY 10018
800-666-9333
www.msccruises.com

NORWEGIAN COASTAL VOYAGES/BERGEN LINE SERVICES
405 Park Avenue
New York, NY 10022
800-323-7436
www.coastalvoyage.com

NORWEGIAN CRUISE LINE
7665 Corporate Center Drive
Miami, FL 33126
800-327-7030
www.ncl.com

OCEANIA CRUISES
8120 NW 53rd Street
Miami, FL 33166
800-531-5619
www.oceaniacruises.com

ODYSSEY CRUISES
401 E. Illinois
Suite 425
Chicago, IL 60611
800-946-7245
www.odysseycruises.com

ORIENT LINES
7665 Corporate Center Drive
Miami, FL 33126
800-333-7300
www.orientlines.com

PETER DEILMANN CRUISES
1800 Diagonal Road
Suite 170
Alexandria, VA 22314
800-348-8287
www.deilmann-cruises.com

PRINCESS CRUISES
24844 Avenue Rockefeller
Santa Clarita, CA 91355
800-774-6237
www.princesscruises.com

RESIDENSEA
5200 Blue Lagoon Drive
Suite 790
Miami, FL 33126
305-264-9090
www.residensea.com

ROYAL CARIBBEAN INTERNATIONAL
1050 Caribbean Way
Miami, FL 33132-2096
800-327-6700
www.rccl.com

ROYAL OLYMPIC CRUISES
805 Third Avenue
18th Floor
New York, NY 10022
800-872-6400
www.royalolympiccruises.com

SEABOURN CRUISE LINE
6100 Blue Lagoon Drive
Suite 400
Miami, FL 33126
800-929-9391
www.seabourn.com

SEADREAM YACHT CLUB
2601 S. Bayshore Drive
Penthouse 1-B
Coconut Grove, FL 33133
800-707-4911
www.seadreamyachtclub.com

SEVEN SEAS CRUISES
600 Corporate Drive
Suite 410
Fort Lauderdale, FL 33334
800-285-1835
www.rssc.com

SILVERSEA CRUISES
110 E. Broward Boulevard
Fort Lauderdale, FL 33301
800-722-9955
www.silversea.com

SPIRIT CRUISES
5700 Lake Wright Drive
Suite 203
Norfolk, VA 23502
757-627-2900
www.spiritcruises.com

STAR CLIPPERS
4101 Salzedo Street
Coral Gables, FL 33146
800-442-0551
www.starclippers.com

STAR CRUISES
7665 Corporate Center Drive
Miami, FL 33126
800-327-9020
www.starcruises.com

SWAN HELLENIC CRUISES
631 Commack Road
Suite 1-A
Commack, NY 11725
877-800-7926
www.swanhellenic.com

UNIWORLD
17323 Ventura Boulevard
Encino, CA 91316
800-733-7820
www.uniworld.com

VIKING RIVER CRUISES
21820 Burbank Boulevard
Suite 100
Woodland Hills, CA 91367
877-66-VIKING
www.vikingrivercruises.com

WINDJAMMER BAREFOOT CRUISES
1759 Bay Road
Miami Beach, FL 33139
800-327-2601
www.windjammer.com

WINDSTAR CRUISES
300 Elliott Avenue West
Seattle, WA 98119
800-258-7245
www.windstarcruises.com

WORLD YACHT DINING CRUISES
Pier 81
W. 41st Street & Hudson River
New York, NY 10036
800-498-4271
www.worldyacht.com

YANKEE FLEET
75 Essex Avenue
Gloucester, MA   01930
800-942-5464
www.yankeefleet.com

ZEUS TOURS & YACHT CRUISES
120 Sylvan Avenue
Englewood Cliffs, NJ   07632
800-447-5667
www.zeustours.com

chapter five:
Tours

Many business trips and vacations begin piecemeal. First, you buy an airline ticket, then you find a hotel room and a rental car, add theme park tickets and restaurant reservations, and....

Tour operators, however, specialize in the entire trip. They sell prepackaged, prepaid itineraries that include transportation (air, sea, or ground), accommodations, meals, admissions, sightseeing guides, and other travel services. These companies promote their packages as saving time and money for travelers who might otherwise book these trip components separately.

Growing from their past low-rent images of weary travelers on aged busses following an *If it's Tuesday, this must be Belgium* schedule, many U.S. tour companies now appeal to a much broader range of passengers. Along with the tour operators that sell basic escorted trips to all segments of the traveling public, you will find many specialist companies that focus on certain destinations (for example, Hawaii, France, or New England) or on types of travelers (such as students, singles, or church groups).

Almost every tour operator concentrates on escorted vacations. These are prearranged trips complete with tour escorts or guides for customers who follow the itinerary together in preformed groups, such as the members of a garden club, or unrelated customers who simply purchased the same tour package. However, more tour companies now also offer independent tours (sometimes called *FIT tours* after an outdated industry term, *Foreign Independent Traveler*), in which the operator pre-arranged the elements of the trip (such as airline tickets and hotel reservations) for singles or couples who then complete the itinerary on their own.

MAKING RESERVATIONS

While travel agents sell approximately 25% of the tour packages sold in the United States, many consumers purchase trips directly from tour companies or online websites. When booking any tour package, it is extremely critical—more so than in other segments of the travel industry—that you investigate the financial condition of the tour company. First, ask your travel agent or the tour company sales representative if the operator carries any type of performance bond that covers its default or bankruptcy. If it does, confirm the amount of the bond. (Remember—the larger the tour company, the more substantial its bond must be in order to cover the tour deposits of all consumers scheduled to travel at any given time.)

Second, ask whether the tour operator deposits consumer payments in an *escrow account*—a bank account separate from the company's own operating account—in which customers' payments are held until the trip actually begins. If so, get the account details from the tour company and contact the bank directly to confirm that, indeed, the escrow account exists and remains in use. Insist that you make your tour payment directly into the escrow account, rather than sending the check made payable to the tour company itself.

Example:

Make the check made payable to "ABC Tours Consumer Escrow" rather than "ABC Tours."

Escrow accounts ensure that tour companies do not depend on your trip payments (largely destined to be paid in turn to the travel suppliers providing the components of your tour) for operating cash flow—a classic mistake that is probably the leading cause of tour operator defaults.

Tour Company Trade Associations

Another line of defense is choosing a tour operator that belongs to one (or both) of the existing consumer protection programs organized by tour company trade associations. Through these programs—offered by the *U.S. Tour Operators Association* (USTOA) and the *CrossSphere*—the tour company must post a performance bond, deposit a required amount of money or letter of credit, or meet other financial criteria to pay back consumers who stand to lose their tour payments if the company goes bankrupt. In that event, you would file a claim with the association to recover your funds from its program. Currently, the USTOA plan offers $5 million in coverage for each of its members, while the NTA plan offers $250,000 in coverage.

Keep in mind, however, that during peak travel seasons, many large tour operators may have deposits on hand well in excess of these limits, meaning that you might still receive only a portion of your money. Another caveat is that these consumer protection plans only pay when the tour operator has entered bankruptcy (not simply ceased operations). Therefore, if a USTOA or CrossSphere member has shut its doors without technically filing for bankruptcy, you may need to contact the court about supporting a legal filing to force the operator into bankruptcy.

Travel Tip

If you have any questions or concerns regarding your tour operator, contact either of the following trade associations:

U.S. Tour Operators Association (USTOA)
275 Madison Avenue
Suite 2014
New York, NY 10016
212-599-6599
212-599-6744 (fax)
www.ustoa.com

CrossSphere
546 E. Main St.
Lexington, KY 40508
859-226-4444
859-226-4414 (fax)
www.crosssphere.com

Even if the tour company displays an association logo in its brochures and materials or advertises that it participates in one or both of these consumer protection plans, you must always confirm at the time you book your trip that the operator is a member *in good standing*. It is not unusual for a tour operator to drop out of its association (or to be removed from membership) long after its brochures have been printed, especially if it is facing fresh financial troubles.

Credit Cards

Another excellent way to protect your tour payments is using a major credit card whenever possible. If a tour company ceases operations or declares bankruptcy, you may be able (under the U.S. *Fair Credit Billing Act*) to request a chargeback on your credit card—in effect, a refund—while the issuing bank for your card investigates what happened. Though the law technically requires you to file a written chargeback request within sixty days of the date on which the tour company charge appears on your credit card bill, some credit card issuers have extended that deadline to 120 days. In the case of travel deposits, some issuing banks are even more understanding about charge back requests. Contact your credit card company, directly, to ask about its charge back policies that apply specifically to travel services.

Travel Insurance

Since the September 11 tragedy, the sale of travel insurance— policies purchased by travelers to cover them in the event of losses due to trip cancellation and delay, luggage problems, and other travel emergencies—has increased tremendously. Many (but definitely not all) travel insurance policies cover you in the event of a travel supplier's default or bankruptcy. Be sure to check the fine print of your policy at the time of purchase, because some companies have introduced major loopholes in their coverage. (For example, your travel insurer might actually have a list of suppliers for which it will not extend bankruptcy coverage, a practice that has grown more common since September 11.)

Never buy insurance directly from the tour company itself. These *self-funded plans* will likely be dissolved if the tour company, itself, goes out of business. Instead, ask for *third-party insurance* from a travel agent or travel insurer.

Seller of Travel Laws

Finally, more than a dozen states now have *seller of travel laws* that regulate travel agents and tour companies. Generally, they require companies that sell travel to register with a state agency. Sometimes, they also mandate the posting of a performance bond (the highest is $50,000 in Nevada) or an escrow account for tour passengers' payments. California has the country's most complex seller of travel law, including a statewide restitution fund that pays consumers under certain conditions if a tour company fails.

Note: *While all of these laws apply to travel agencies, tour operators have lobbied successfully for exemptions in some jurisdictions.*

To find out whether a specific tour operator falls under any state seller of travel law, contact the attorney general's office in both the state where you live and the state in which the tour company is headquartered.

PROBLEMS WITH THE TOUR

It almost never pays to sue a tour operator unless there is a major factual difference between the trip promised before you depart and the actual tour you experienced. The actual damage awards will likely be much smaller than your out-of-pocket legal expenses.

In many cases, your best recourse if there is a factual discrepancy—for example, the tour stopped at tourist-class hotels instead of the five-star resorts promised in the brochures—is demanding a partial refund or other compensation from the tour operator. You should present your complaint to the tour company's representatives (such as the tour escort or guide) when the problem arises during the tour, and (if possible) submit your complaint in writing, even if it is a handwritten note on hotel stationery. Also, take photographs or video footage that support your complaint so that you have a visual record of the problem.

Once the tour is underway, you might encounter any number of common concerns about packaged trips. The tour company may change the itinerary after you have departed, skipping a stop or substituting one city for another. The tour guide may ask you to change accommodations if the hotel is oversold. You may find that your accommodations are uncomfortable, unsanitary, or unsafe. Sometimes, the tour company may reschedule the entire tour or cancel the trip altogether.

Itinerary Changes

In their brochures and ads, as well as the trip contracts, most tour companies post notices indicating they reserve the right to make changes and substitutions in your itinerary whenever it is necessary. Generally, these clauses also say that the operator is not required to give you any advance warning about the changes and you need to simply go with the flow on minor changes. However, if the operator makes substantial changes in the promised itinerary to the point that you cannot enjoy the trip for which you paid (or you believe the changes make your tour worth less than you paid for it), then you may have grounds to claim breach of contract or misrepresentation on the part of the tour company.

The most common change in tour itineraries is hotel substitutions. If the tour company makes wholesale switches in hotels for your tour, and you believe that the new hotels are less desirable or lower in quality than the hotels promised in the itinerary when you purchased the tour, you should be able to ask the tour operator for a partial refund or other compensation.

Some tour operators will notify you before your departure if changes have been made in the itinerary. If the changes concern you, definitely contact the company immediately to request a partial refund, a complete refund and cancellation of your reservation, or alternate arrangements for you (such as being placed in the original hotels, rather than the substitutes). Your bargaining position is much stronger *before* the tour departs. Otherwise, if you take the tour but complain about the advance changes afterwards, the tour company will rightfully claim that you were notified of the changes and decided to take the tour anyway.

If you learn about changes once the tour is underway, you should speak with the tour leader or guide and voice your concerns immediately. If possible, you should present your concerns in writing, even if it is simply a handwritten note at the time. Tell the tour company representative that you want an immediate effort to correct the problem.

Again, you should remember that your best bargaining position is raising a complaint on the spot, rather than addressing the issue when you return home. You must decide whether the changes that have been announced are indeed substantial enough to interrupt your vacation with a complaint. Because tour programs may be designed years in advance of the actual trip, it is inevitable that some details of the itinerary may change (for example, individual hotel properties may have closed since the tour was planned, or road conditions may have worsened due to unpredictably bad weather).

Travel Advisories

Changes made by outside parties—especially governments—raise interesting questions. After September 11, some travelers found themselves facing brand-new travel advisories and warnings issued by the U.S. State Department for tours that had been booked months in advance. Generally, tour company contracts include disclaimers that the operator is not responsible in the event of travel advisories or warnings issued by government agencies (as well as government-mandated changes in itineraries, such as the closing of a national monument). As a consumer, you may be left in a tough spot, as it will be next to impossible to recover damages against a government agency for changes in your tour plans. Some travel insurance policies do cover you if you must cancel your trip due to new government restrictions.

Check the fine print in your policy for details. Many reputable tour companies have begun offering less restrictive cancellation policies for travelers who are concerned about ongoing threats of war or terrorism.

INJURIES

Whether you hurt yourself stepping down from the tour bus or tumbling over rocks in your kayak during a river ecotour, physical injuries have become more common as tour packages grow in popularity. If you believe the tour operator is at fault for your injury, the first question in trying to recover damages from the company is whether it has any official business location or connection within the United States.

It is extremely difficult and expensive to attempt to pursue a physical injury lawsuit against a tour operator based in another country. If you sustain an injury while taking a packaged trip outside the U.S.A. with a tour operator that has no U.S. locations or connections (for instance, you purchased a sightseeing day tour in Paris upon arriving in that city), then you will likely have to settle for filing a claim with your health insurance and travel insurance carriers.

Additionally, there are several daunting obstacles to filing a personal injury lawsuit against any tour operator. First, most parts of your tour package—the flights, hotel stays, meals, admissions, bus rides, etc.—are actually provided by independent travel suppliers, not the tour operator directly. The tour operator acts as an agent for these companies, assembling their services into packages for travelers to buy. In other words, the tour operator is an independent contractor, and most U.S. courts will not hold an agent or independent contractor responsible for problems caused by *principals* (the airlines, hotel companies, or other suppliers who actually provide the services to you). In these cases, you will have to consider targeting instead the travel supplier responsible for the component of the trip on which you sustained your injury.

Second, many tour operators require their customers to sign consumer disclaimer notices, trip waivers, and contract terms in order to reserve space on a trip. By signing these disclaimers and waivers, you typically agree to release the tour operator from any liability for injuries or damages while you are on the trip. Some forms require you to assume all risks, whether the injury or damage is caused by the tour operator, its agents or employees, or any independent parties such as travel suppliers.

In the past, the courts did not always uphold these restrictive contract terms. The myth began that travel disclaimers are rarely enforced. However, many tour operators have strengthened their disclaimers in recent years, especially for higher risk trips such as student spring break tours and adventure ecotours. Do not sign any disclaimer, waiver, or contract provision offered by the tour operator without the understanding that you are signing a binding legal document. Always read the form carefully and decide whether you can live with the terms being imposed upon you before you sign it.

Sometimes, tour operators do have direct responsibility for your damages or injuries. For example, some tour companies have purchased their own hotels, motorcoaches, or other assets that they use in their own packaged trips. In these cases, the tour company would be liable for your injuries under at least the same standards as typical owners of hotels, motorcoaches, and other travel services.

Vicarious Responsibility

Tour operators may also incur *vicarious responsibility* for the actions of other parties that led to your injuries. First, the company may cut corners in planning and operating the tour in a way that it knows (or should know) will increase the risks of injury to passengers, leading to claims of negligence on its part.

For example, the operator may plan its National Parks in the Southwestern U.S. itinerary through a more desolate stretch of desert with fewer roadside services in order to cut motorcoach costs, with the knowledge that (with an older crowd of passengers on board) there is little help available if an emergency occurs during the trip. The operator may also be negligent in selecting qualified, professional travel suppliers for the trip. In the competitive travel industry, tour companies have a wide selection of suppliers for most travel services. Therefore, if they select a company that falls down on its part of the job, the tour operator itself may be judged negligent in picking the supplier (especially if the motivation is cutting costs).

Another arena of vicarious responsibility lies with the tour operator's personnel. The company must provide employees (particularly tour guides and drivers) who will not expose you to unreasonable risk, unless the risk is an inherent part of the trip. In a noted case, the court ruled against a tour company in Israel and its guide who led an American tourist onto a path marked *off limits*. The tourist suffered brain damage from a serious injury received on the off-limits path and recovered a substantial award from the tour company for negligence. If the tour company advertises having *professional guides* and *expert staff*, it must be able to support those claims about its employees and independent contractors. You may succeed in basing your personal injury claim on inexperienced tour personnel, saying that you would not have taken the trip if you had known the claims of professionalism were false.

Sometimes, tour companies (or suppliers acting as tour companies, such as hotels and airlines) create a false sense of security by incorporating famous brand names into their materials for passengers, making it seem as if the bigger company has control over the tour operation. Another famous case involved a U.S. couple who took a tour in Italy that included a rental car from a business using the Hertz name. After they were injured in an accident in the car, they successfully sued Hertz. They argued that, because they saw the Hertz name in their tour materials, they reasonably relied upon the reputation of Hertz's parent company in the U.S.

(even though Hertz did not own the rental car or the Italian franchise from which the couple picked up the car).

Watch especially for phrases in the tour operator's materials that imply ownership or partnership in brand-name suppliers. If you book the tour based on that reputation, but find much lower standards of care and quality on the trip, you may argue successfully that the tour company gave you misleading information upon which you made your tour purchase.

Finally, the tour operator may incur vicarious responsibility by breaching its *warrant of safety*, making statements in its ads that play down any risks of the tour in order to persuade travelers to take the trip. If the tour turns out to be dangerous, you can claim negligence on the part of the tour operator (even if you signed a waiver) because you relied on the company's promises of safety. In one case, the tour operator offered diving trips to Costa Rica with the following statement in its brochure: "[The] safety and comfort of our clientele is always foremost, and we will do everything in our power to ensure the same." Even though the tour company was not directly responsible for the injuries that occurred on the trip, the court found the U.S.-based tour company vicariously liable for the negligence of its Costa Rican dive suppliers (who escaped liability in the U.S. legal system).

Intentional Injuries

Though it happens very rarely, a tour company or its employees or contractors may intentionally harm a passenger. If the company itself commits the crime, its action would render useless any waiver or disclaimer signed by the traveler. If the company's employee or agent carried out the act, the company may be able to protect itself by claiming it is not liable for the unforeseen, *intervening and illegal* acts of a third party. However, if the tour operator could have reasonably foreseen the actions (for example, the employee had been guilty of assault in the past), then the company may be liable for negligent supervision.

BANKRUPT OPERATORS

In the 1990s, the travel industry witnessed a rash of defaults, bankruptcies, and closings by tour operators—not just small mom and pop operators, but several multi-million-dollar tour companies with thousands of clients apiece. Some companies literally shut their doors overnight, leaving tour groups stranded at destinations mid-trip and other consumers holding tour documents and vouchers that were worthless because the travel suppliers involved in the tour (airlines, hotels, motor-coach companies, and other services) had not been paid by the tour company.

You are a creditor of the tour company when it declares bankruptcy—in line to receive reimbursement for your tour deposit and final payments once the operator's assets have been liquidated. Practice has proved, however, that consumers generally receive next to nothing as major creditors—travel suppliers, banks, and lawyers—take their share of the assets at the front of the line. If consumers do receive any payout from the operator's bankruptcy estate, the process can take years before a check arrives in the mail.

What are the most common warning signs that a tour operator is in financial hot water? Beware of companies offering huge last-minute discounts and deals that are well below the prices of competing tour operators, especially if they require substantial deposits or full payment well in advance of the tour's departure date or refuse to accept credit cards for payments. Unfortunately, you cannot place much weight on the tour company's business history, as the 1990s saw the demise of several major, well-respected tour companies that had been in business for decades.

CHARTERED PACKAGES

Additional federal regulations apply when you purchase a tour package that includes charter air service or event tickets (such as the Olympics, the World Series, or college football games). Before tour operators promote *public charters*, they (or the charter airline, depending on the structure of the tour package) must file a prospectus with the *U.S. Department of Transportation* (DOT) for every single package before it can be offered for sale to the public. The prospectus must also include the name of the airline that will operate the charter flight and the names of all hotels that are part of the package. The prospectus must also confirm that the company has set up a *security agreement*—usually, a surety bond or escrow account—in order to protect customers' payments. The tour operator must also tell the DOT in the prospectus whether event tickets will be offered as part of the package.

Once the DOT has reviewed the prospectus and approved it, the DOT Public Charter Office issues the package a *PC* reference number, confirming that the company has met the federal requirements for selling the trip. Therefore, always ask the travel agent or tour operator for the PC number when you are considering any charter package. (You can also check with the Public Charter Office directly at 202-366-2396.)

DOT regulations also require tour companies to have a significant number of actual tickets in hand before promoting or selling any special events package. As an alternative, the operator may present the DOT a copy of its written ticket purchase agreement or contract with the event organizers or a ticket wholesaler. If a tour company accepts payments for a trip without tickets or a contract as required, it must refund payments to customers within three days.

Sometimes, the tour operator will ask you to sign a waiver (permitted under DOT rules) confirming that you understand that no tickets will be provided as part of the package. If you agree that you did not expect the company to provide tickets, then you may consider signing the waiver.

Finally, customers may cancel their reservations and receive a full refund within fourteen days of any unexpected package price increases more than 10% above the previously announced price. Also, the company is never allowed to increase the package price less than ten days before the initial flight.

(You may request an official copy of these DOT regulations by calling 202-366-2220.)

chapter six:
International Travel

"Traveling is the ruin of all happiness!" English novelist Fanny Burney declared in his 1782 novel *Cecilia*. "There's no looking at a building here after seeing Italy."

Despite the latest rounds of war and terrorism, many Americans still feel that way about traveling abroad. Each year, more than 40 million trips outside U.S. borders to other countries—nearly one overseas trip for every seven Americans.

When you leave the United States, for the most part you will lie beyond the standard protections that American citizens sometimes take for granted. While this book cannot explain the local laws and customs of every nation to which you may travel, this chapter describes the basic steps you can take to prepare yourself for international travel and to avoid common troubles abroad.

YOUR KEY U.S. DOCUMENTS

When you travel outside the United States, the most basic official document you will need is a current U.S. passport. Though you can travel to adjoining countries like Canada and Mexico and to some Caribbean countries with only your birth certificate and other forms of government identification (for example, your driver's license or your Social Security card), the U.S. passport remains the primary proof of citizenship that you can carry as a traveler.

To apply for your very first passport, you should appear in person at any one of more than 5,000 U.S. courthouses and post offices that have been specifically authorized to accept passport applications. (Call the general switchboard number at the courthouse or post office to ask whether that location is approved for passport applications.) If you need your passport urgently (that is, if you are traveling abroad within two weeks), you may contact any of the thirteen U.S. passport agencies around the country (Boston, Chicago, Honolulu, Houston, Los Angeles, Miami, New Orleans, New York, Norwalk (Conn.), Philadelphia, San Francisco, Seattle, and Washington, D.C.) that accept applications by appointment. You must call the passport agency in advance, and you may be asked to provide proof that you have the urgent need for a passport (such as your airline ticket showing travel within the next fourteen days).

If you were born in the United States, you should bring with you an official certified copy of your birth certificate. If you do not have one, you can request a copy from the agency that records births or vital statistics in the state in which you were born, usually for a nominal fee.

Travel Tip

Unless you've waited absolutely too late to apply through normal channels, think twice about using expediting firms to handle your passport or visa application. They're very expensive ($150-$250), and you can avoid the need for expediting if you plan ahead to request these documents.

If you cannot secure a copy of your birth certificate for some reason, you will need instead a *letter of no record* issued by your state with your name, date of birth, and a statement showing the years that were searched for your birth record and the fact that there is no birth certificate on file for you. Along with the letter of record, you must bring as many other proofs of birth as possible, including baptismal certificates, hospital birth certificates, census records, early school records, family Bible records, or your doctor's record of postnatal care. You may also submit a notarized affidavit of birth signed by an older blood relative who has personal knowledge of your birth.

If you were born outside the United States, you will need a copy of the consular report of birth abroad or certification of birth, your naturalization certificate, or your citizenship certificate as proof of your U.S. citizenship.

Also, you will need proof of your identity—a valid driver's license, a government or military ID card, or a certificate of naturalization or citizenship. If these are not available, you may bring other *signature documents* such as a Social Security card or credit card, along with a person who can vouch for you who does have valid identification. Finally, bring two identical 2" x 2" photographs taken within the past six months (color or black and white, front view, full face, on a light background).

Plan to apply for your passport at least 90 days in advance of your trip. (State Department officials say six weeks, but you should not cut corners.) You may pay an additional fee of $60 for expedited service (two weeks' turnaround). If you plan to travel overseas a lot, you should ask for a larger, 48-page passport for no extra charge.

Know Before You Go

The busiest months for passport applications and renewals are April and May.

Children

Recent legislation changed the procedures for minors seeking U.S. passports. Children ages 14 to 17 must appear in person to apply for a passport and, if the child does not have identification of his or her own, a parent must accompany the child, present identification, and co-sign the application.

Children under the age of 14 do not routinely need to appear in person to apply for a passport. However, the application requires consent from both parents or legal guardians, in an effort to prevent the child's unauthorized removal from the U.S.

in any custody battle. Both parents or guardians must present current, valid identification, and the application must include additional documents showing the child's custody or guardianship arrangements. For more details, check **http://travel.state.gov**. (Concerned parents may also request that their child's name be entered in the State Department's passport name-check system. This system notifies parents if passport applications are made on behalf of their children. For more details, call 202-736-7000.)

If the child is too young to sign the passport, a parent should print the child's name and sign his or her own name inside the child's passport, writing the word "father" or "mother" beside the signature.

The current fees for initial passports are $80 for adults (valid for 10 years) and $70 for children under the age of 16 (valid for five years). The renewal fee is $55.

Passport Renewals and Changes

Once your initial passport expires, you may renew it by mail if you received it within the past 15 years; you were over the age of 16 when it was issued; and, you still have the same legal name that appears in the passport. When the State Department sends you the renewed passport, it will also return to you the old, canceled passport. Keep it in a safe place, as it is considered proof of U.S. citizenship. Try to renew your passport at least nine months before it expires, as some countries will not permit you to enter if your passport is set to expire in less than six months. If you return to the U.S. after your passport expired while you were out of the country, the *U.S. Citizenship and Naturalization Services* (USCIS) will likely fine you when you reenter.

If you wish to change your name on your valid U.S. passport (for example, if you are now divorced and using your maiden name), you must file a form with the State Department. The form should be accompanied by your current passport and a certified copy of your marriage certificate, divorce papers, or name change court decree.

You will find more information about passports, including downloadable application forms, at **http://travel.state.gov**. You may also call the *National Passport Information Center* at 877-487-2778.

Noncitizens

If you are not a U.S. citizen, you must carry a valid passport from the country in which you hold citizenship. Even if you carry a *green card*, a visa, or any other type of permit to live in the United States, you may not legally hold a U.S. passport if you are not an American citizen. When you leave the United States to enter another country abroad, you will be bound by the rules that your destination country applies to travelers from the country in which you hold citizenship, not the United States. For example, if you are a citizen of Spain living in the U.S. on a student visa and you decide to travel to Ecuador for a vacation, you must meet all of the limits and restrictions imposed by Ecuador on Spanish citizens entering its borders. Along the same lines, you should contact the nearest USCIS office before you leave the United States to find out if you should carry with you any other documents besides your country's passport (*e.g.,* your *green card*) so that you can avoid delays or challenges when you reenter the U.S. at the end of your trip abroad.

ENTRY REQUIREMENTS OF FOREIGN COUNTRIES

Many nations require U.S. citizens to apply for a visa—typically, a stamp or sticker placed directly on a page inside the passport—before entering their borders. The visa represents official government permission to visit for a certain number of days or for a specific purpose. Through the U.S. government's popular *Visa Waiver Program*, many countries in Europe and the Caribbean no longer require visas for U.S. citizens arriving on business or leisure trips lasting no longer than thirty days.

Generally, you must apply for any required visa by mail from the foreign government's U.S. consulates (on rare occasions, you will be asked to appear in person), and you must pay a fee that varies widely depending on the country, your purpose for traveling, and your planned length of stay. (The consulate may also request a passport-sized photograph, so you should consider asking for extra copies when you have your passport photographs made.) As with your passport, allow plenty of time—a minimum of thirty days if possible—to apply by mail for a required visa.

In the past, you could sometimes delay securing your visa until you actually arrived in the foreign country. With tougher security measures today, however, you will likely be barred from boarding the airplane for your destination without the visa in place (and, even if you make the flight, you may be deported immediately when you arrive on the next available flight back to the United States). Some countries still accept tourist cards issued by airlines and travel agents, but they are not always a perfect substitute for a visa, so it is best to apply for an actual visa whenever possible.

Even with a valid visa, some nations have additional entry requirements to prove that you will not cause trouble during your stay, such as:

- a valid round-trip airline ticket (proving that you plan to leave the country at some point to return to the U.S.);
- adequate funds or credit cards (proving that you will not need to seek employment to survive);
- a valid hotel reservation or other place to stay;
- immunization or health certificates; or,
- a letter from your company (if you are traveling on business) explaining the purpose for your trip.

In isolated instances, the country's immigration officials may require you to change a minimum amount of U.S. dollars into the local currency immediately upon entering. On other occasions, they may refuse to admit U.S. travelers whose long hair or inappropriate clothing is not acceptable in the foreign country's culture (for example, mini skirts in some Muslim nations). There is little room to mount any effective argument at the arrival airport. If you do not adhere to these rules, you will simply not be allowed to enter the country.

Do not rely solely on your travel agent, the airline, your tour operator, or any other secondary sources, as they may have outdated information on the entry requirements for other countries. You should always personally contact the nearest U.S. embassy or consulate of the country you are planning to visit, as well as the U.S. State Department's website at **http://travelregistration.state.gov/ibrs**. (The State Department also publishes Consular Information Sheets for any overseas country containing helpful information beyond simply the entry requirements.) Keep in mind that travel agents have no obligation to give you information about entry requirements in most cases. Many travel suppliers have clauses in their tickets and brochures specifically relieving them of any such obligations.

TRAVEL ADVISORIES AND PROHIBITIONS

Beyond its Consular Information Sheets, the State Department also issues various levels of warnings and advisories about countries that it believes pose a significant hazard for traveling Americans (physical danger, detainment and arrest, serious health hazards, crime, terrorism, political unrest, and other troubles). Dangers that are not severe enough to justify a full-blown warning are generally issued as *travel advisories*.

On the other hand, *travel warnings* result from a definite pattern of risks in the selected country that could lead to harm for U.S. travelers. Wars, epidemics, natural disasters, prolonged labor strikes, or severe political unrest are the most common factors contributing to a travel warning. If the State Department issues a travel warning, it will stay in effect until federal officials believe the dangers have passed. Many travel suppliers will consider canceling trips to that nation when a travel warning is issued. You may find that your travel insurance coverage does not extend after that date if you choose to proceed with your trip. (The State Department posts a complete list of current travel warnings in effect at **http://travel.state.gov/travel** and click "Current Warnings."

In the most extreme cases, the U.S. government has imposed severe travel restrictions or even a complete travel ban for certain countries where the threat to American travelers is considered enormous. Countries currently banned include:

- Afghanistan;
- Iran;
- Iraq;
- Lebanon;
- Libya; and,
- North Korea.

Under the U.S. *Trading With the Enemy Act*, only travelers such as journalists, researchers, and people with close relatives are allowed to obtain licenses to travel to Cuba. The State Department strongly discourages travel to any country with which the U.S. government does not maintain diplomatic relations. If you choose to take a trip to one of these nations, you will be unable to rely on almost any level of help from U.S. officials if you encounter difficulties on your trip.

HEALTH ISSUES

You will be required to provide proof that you have been immunized against certain communicable diseases such as cholera or tuberculosis before you enter some countries. Once you have been vaccinated, your doctor can give you an international certificate of vaccination approved by the *World Health Organization*. Some countries now also require additional medical exams, such as testing for HIV, if you plan to stay longer than a few weeks. In other cases, you should voluntarily be vaccinated against illnesses that are common in your destination. The *U.S. Centers for Disease Control and Prevention* provides updates on required vaccinations. You can contact them at **www.cdc.gov** or 800-311-3435.

You can request the booklets *Health Information for International Travel* or *International Certificates of Vaccination* from the Superintendent of Documents, U.S. Government Printing Office, Washington, D.C. 20402. The cost is $6 for the first publication and $2 for the second one.

Many U.S. health insurance policies do not cover any medical expenses that you may incur while traveling abroad, so you should check your own policy for any limitations before you leave the United States. If your existing policy does not cover non-U.S. treatment, ask about get-

> ### Travel Tip
>
> Do not bring back any viruses as souvenirs. Get a flu shot before you go abroad, wash your hands regularly (and carry antibacterial towelettes), drink plenty of water (but not tap), and take a multivitamin daily.

ting a rider on your policy for overseas travel or purchase short-term coverage such as a travel insurance policy. Also, consider whether you need emergency medical transportation coverage in the event that you must be transported back to the United States for medical care. (See Chapter 8 for details.)

Drugs

Given the global war on drugs, many nations now have very strict policies prohibiting the import and use of drugs, even those for which you have a valid prescription. Always carry any prescription medications with you in your carry-on luggage in their original labeled containers. If you are taking certain medicines such as sleeping pills or pain killers, they may be illegal in some countries even though you have a prescription. Check with your travel agent, travel supplier, or the country's U.S. embassy or consulate before taking them with you on the trip. You might consider carrying a note from your doctor on his or her letterhead, as well as the prescription bottle itself, for such drugs.

Also, some common over-the-counter remedies such as non-prescription sleeping pills may also be banned in certain countries, so you should always leave such drugs in their original labeled containers.

Note: *Bring enough medication to last your entire trip, as many common U.S. drugs may not be readily available overseas.*

BASIC ISSUES TRAVELING ABROAD

Despite what popular movies may suggest, you carry no additional rights as a U.S. citizen when you travel in other countries. Inside the borders of another nation, you must obey that country's laws. Ignorance of those laws is never an excuse. In fact, anti-American sentiment has continued to swell in many corners of the world after September 11 and the U.S. skirmishes with Iraq and North Korea. Personal freedoms that Americans take for granted—such as the rights to free speech, assembly, and attorney representation—do not exist in many other countries. Actions that are legal in the U.S. can lead to arrest and jail in other countries.

Identification

While you are traveling outside the United States, your passport will remain your primary means of official identification. Always keep it in a very secure place. Check twice each time that you remove it from your pocket or purse to ensure that you have returned it safely.

Almost 30,000 U.S. passports are lost or stolen overseas every year. To avoid delays if this happens to you, make two photocopies of the passport pages that show your picture and signature. Keep one set of copies at your home in the U.S. (or, if you live alone, with a relative), and carry the other set with you on the trip in a place separate from the actual passport. If you need a replacement passport, contact the local police immediately to report your lost or stolen original. Then, proceed to the nearest U.S. embassy or consulate with the photocopied pages and another form of photo ID to request a replacement (or, if time does not allow, a notice of official permission to reenter the U.S. without your passport). If your original passport surfaces after you have gotten a replacement, return the original to the embassy or consulate. If you were issued a temporary passport overseas, return it to the nearest U.S. passport office when you arrive home so that you can be issued an official replacement.

If you lose your passport in the United States, alert the local police and contact the nearest U.S. passport office for a replacement.

Some nations require you to carry photo identification at all times. While your passport is an excellent means of identification, you might consider leaving it in your hotel (preferably, the hotel safe) and carrying a photocopy of the passport pages along with your valid driver's license or other photo ID card, to avoid the risk of your passport being stolen. Explain to the authorities if you are stopped that the original passport is stored in your hotel safe.

Local Laws

You should steer clear of any involvement with illegal drugs, as the penalties for possessing even tiny quantities of marijuana, cocaine, and other narcotics can be especially severe (including sentences of hard labor or death).

Immigration officials and police officers in other countries generally have full rein to inspect any books, magazines, photographs, computer disks, videotapes, and personal papers you may have when you enter or leave their borders. In some conservative nations, any documents or pictures considered pornographic or blasphemous could cause

Know Before You Go

Beware of strict limits in some countries on taking photographs—especially shots of government buildings, airports, and military installations (as well as strikes, riots, and other civil unrest). Your camera and film could be confiscated, and you might be jailed. When in doubt, ask officials before you take the picture.

you trouble. Be especially careful in carrying any local papers that might be considered seditious, such as pamphlets given out on the street by demonstrators.

Some countries enforce rules governing personal appearance and behavior that many U.S. travelers will resent, but you must obey them or risk punishment. For example, Singapore prohibits chewing gum in public and Myanmar prohibits traveling with a backpack.

If you are arrested in another country, you should immediately tell the police that you are an American citizen and ask that the nearest U.S. consulate be contacted immediately. While the U.S. consular officers cannot secure your release from jail, they can check on your condition in jail, refer you to local English-speaking attorneys, tell your friends and family about your arrest (if you wish), and set up transfers of money, food, and clothing.

Note: *Because you are not being held in an American jail you do not have the same civil rights (such as Miranda warnings about remaining silent or quick access to an attorney). Be extremely careful about what you say to local authorities, and prepare yourself for any anti-American sentiment that may come your way.*

Currency

Do not plan to carry large amounts of local currency into or out of a country without asking about the local currency control laws. (You must complete U.S. Customs Form 4790 if you plan to carry more than $10,000 in U.S. currency or negotiable instruments such as stocks or bonds.) Also, avoid changing currency in another country at any outlet except your hotel, a post office, a bank, or a government agency, as you may fall victim to scam artists giving you outdated currency or charging you an extremely high exchange rate.

Using your credit card or debit card abroad is an excellent means of avoiding exchange problems, and you will likely receive a much better exchange rate from your bank. Beware of hidden charges by some U.S. credit card issuers for using your card abroad. (Ask your bank about any such charges, and see Chapter 8 for more details.)

Getting Help

A good source of help for Americans traveling outside the U.S. is the *American Citizen Services and Crisis Management* (ACSCM) division of the State Department. As the official communications network for U.S. consulates in other countries, ACSCM fields approximately 14,000 emergency calls, messages, and money transfers annually between Americans who have had accidents, gotten sick, been arrested, lost their money, or died, and their families and friends back home. You can contact ACSCM at 202-647-5225 (Monday through Saturday) or 202-634-3600 (Sundays and holidays) or send a fax to 202-647-6201.

RETURNING TO THE UNITED STATES FROM ABROAD

When you return home to the United States from your international trip, you must clear reviews (and, perhaps, inspections) by the *U.S. Customs and Border Protection* (CBP) and by the *U.S. Customs Service* (Customs). CBP enforces federal regulations governing the flow of people arriving in the country, while Customs focuses on the flow of goods entering with them.

If you arrive home by plane, you will leave the aircraft and stand in line to speak with an CBP officer who will check your passport. The officer may also ask you questions about your trip or your identity (for example, *Did you travel for business or pleasure?* or *Where were you born?*). Sometimes, CBP officers will stamp your passport showing the date and location of your return.

Once you have cleared the CBP review, you will claim any checked baggage and proceed to the Customs station. If you return to the U.S. by land (car, R.V., motorcoach) or by sea (cruise ship), many border stations and ports combine the CBP and Customs reviews into a single stop.

Travel Tip

After September 11, the rules changed for locking your luggage and for wrapping your best leather suitcases in plastic at the airport to avoid nicks and dings. The rule of thumb traveling today is using sturdy suitcases that can take punishment—and leave the locks at home. (Airport security officers will literally remove them if they must inspect your bags.)

Your first step at Customs will be filling out a Customs Declaration Form by writing down your contact information and any items that you purchased or were given during your international trip that you are carrying with you. Many airlines, cruise lines, and tour operators will distribute blank Customs Declaration Forms to passengers near the end of your trip, giving you extra time to complete your report. The head of a family may fill out a single form as a joint declaration for all family members who live together in the same household and who are returning to the U.S. at the same time.

Once you have completed the form, you will line up to speak with a Customs officer who will review your declaration, ask you a few questions, and decide whether you may leave or whether your baggage should be inspected. The typical inspection involves opening your luggage in plain sight for a quick look at its contents. However, Customs officers have broad powers to search your luggage and you. It will only delay your exit if you respond in a disruptive manner. These powers include searching your luggage thoroughly (including taking a suitcase apart if needed) as well as items of a personal nature such as your prescriptions, your shaving kit or cosmetics case, and your purse or wallet. Though it happens very rarely, you can file a complaint (but not recover money damages or a replacement) if the Customs inspection destroys your luggage.

If you are tapped for a personal search, Customs officers have the right to conduct a pat down search (and, in only the most extreme cases, a more thorough inspection that might require disrobing). These searches must be done with the approval of a supervisor with two officers present during the search, and officers of the opposite sex may not search you.

Finally, if you miss a connection flight because you were delayed in Customs, you cannot take action against the federal government. Most airlines will put you on the next available flight without penalty if you explain the reason for your delay.

Personal Exemption

Customs regulations give you a *personal exemption* to bring up to $800 worth of purchases or gifts when you return to the United States without paying any duties, taxes, or penalties. The exemption decreases to $600 if you are returning from one of the following Latin American or Caribbean nations: Antigua and Barbuda, Aruba, Bahamas, Barbados, Belize, British Virgin Islands, Costa Rica, Dominica, Dominican Republic, El Salvador, Grenada, Guatemala, Guyana, Honduras, Jamaica, Montserrat, Netherlands Antilles, Nicaragua, Panama, St. Kitts and Nevis, St. Lucia, St. Vincent and the Grenadines, or Trinidad and Tobago. The exemption increases to $1,200 if your destination was a U.S. insular possession such as American Samoa, Guam, or the U.S. Virgin Islands.

To qualify for this exemption, you must:
- have the items in your carry-on or checked baggage;
- list the items on your Customs form;
- have traveled outside the United States more than forty-eight hours (the exception is travel to Mexico);
- have items for your personal or household use; and,
- not have used your personal exemption within the past thirty days.

Keep your sales slips in the event that you are questioned about the actual value of any item.

Limitations and Duties

Certain items carry additional limitations. For example, you can include in your personal exemption no more than 100 cigars or 200 cigarettes and no more than one liter of alcohol. These items may not be included by minors in their exemptions. You may have to pay federal excise taxes or state and local sales taxes on them even if they are exempted from Customs duties.

Also, you may bring back with you free of duty any belongings that you purchased in the U.S. To avoid confusion at the Customs station when you return home with your own video camera, laptop computer, jewelry, or other valuables, you should carry your purchase receipts with you if possible and register these items with Customs (Form CF 4457) before you depart the United States at the beginning of your trip.

Know Before You Go

Items purchased at the duty-free shop are free of duty _only_ in the country where the shop is located. When you return to the U.S., that perfume or those sunglasses will be subject to Customs duties. (Beware of the markups at duty-free shops, too—you can usually find better bargains at discount shops in your final destination.)

If you are charged duty on any items you are bringing back to the United States, understand that the amount of the duty varies according to Customs formulas. (See **www.customs.gov** for full details.) You must pay the duty immediately upon your return, so be prepared if you believe the total value of your purchases or gifts may exceed your personal exemption.

Other items are completely prohibited and you may not bring them back with you for _any_ reason:

- narcotics and dangerous drugs;
- hazardous and toxic materials;
- explosives;
- fireworks;
- endangered species (including any products made with most ivory, crocodile and alligator skins, or sea turtles);

- many plant and animal products;
- pirated copies of software or music;
- trademarked articles;
- some textiles; and,
- cultural property (such as archaeological artifacts).

If you purchase an animal overseas, it is subject to inspection and possible quarantine when you return.

Mail Items Home

While you are traveling overseas, you may ship home packages containing purchases and gifts without paying duty on them, provided that you ship no more than $200 worth of goods in the same day. You may also send up to $100 a day in gifts to any person in the U.S. without paying duty. However, when doing this, you must mark the packages as "unsolicited gifts" and mark the outside with your name, the type of gifts enclosed, their retail value, and the recipient's name. These exemptions may not include alcoholic beverages, any tobacco products (unless the entire package is worth less than $5), or alcohol-based fragrances.

Your shipped packages are subject to inspection by Customs and U.S. Postal Service officials. If you exceed these dollar limits, you will be charged twice the rate of duty. These rules change for items shipped from the U.S. Virgin Islands, American Samoa, Guam, and some nations in the Caribbean. Be sure to check with Customs before you depart.

chapter seven:
Travel Agents, Consolidators, and Websites

Most consumers still choose to arrange their business trips and vacations by working with a professional travel agent. More than 30,000 travel agencies in America (and an estimated 40,000 to 60,000 independent agents who work from their homes) sell 95% of all cruises, 70% of airline tickets, and 30%–40% of car rentals, hotel reservations, and tour packages purchased by U.S. travelers.

In the 1980's, a new type of travel seller became popular—*consolidators* (also called *ticket brokers*) or companies that specialize in selling heavily discounted airline tickets that they have secured from specific carriers in bulk purchasing agreements. The late 1990's saw the rise of a third important type of retailer—travel websites, including both independent online agencies, such as *Travelocity* and *Expedia*, as well as consumer booking sites run by individual airlines and other travel suppliers. Regardless of their structures, these three types of travel sellers—traditional travel agents, airline consolidators, and travel websites—have similar duties and responsibilities toward their clients.

BEFORE YOU BOOK YOUR TRIP
Regardless of which retail channel you choose, take steps to minimize potential problems.

Decide What You Want the Travel Retailer to Do for You

While some consumers simply want ticketing assistance (*e.g., I'm going from Chicago to Los Angeles and I need a cheap ticket on this date*), other travelers need a completely customized travel package, including air, hotel, car rental, theme park tickets, and other services (*e.g. We're taking the kids to Florida—put together a trip for us*). Other consumers view their travel agents as counselors, relying on their recommendations to decide where they should go (*e.g., Give me some ideas about a romantic holiday on an island*).

Generally, the more involved the travel retailer becomes in offering professional recommendations, the greater his or her obligations may become to his or her clients.

Pick a Specialist If you Need One

Many neighborhood travel agencies and travel websites specialize in certain types of travel (honeymoons, rail trips, cruises) or travelers (business people, disabled travelers, grandparents vacationing with their grandchildren). If you have special needs, or a certain type of trip in mind, make sure that you find a retailer who has experience in that niche.

Be Very Specific in Your Requests and Do Not Be Afraid to Ask Questions

Take an active role in planning your travel. If possible, give the retailer your trip requests in writing, and use dates and figures and place names as much as you can. State upfront if you have absolute requirements (for example, the lowest possible airfare regardless of the restrictions) or if you prefer a specific travel supplier. If you have questions about the travel arrangements, it is better to ask before writing your check or boarding the airplane.

Request Details about Your Retailer's Experience and Business Credentials

Specifically, you should ask whether the agent or consolidator or website is licensed, registered, or bonded in your state (fourteen U.S. states now require these sorts of credentials for travel sellers). Most professional travel agencies carry a minimum of $1 million in professional liability/errors and omissions insurance coverage as well. Also, find out if your agent belongs to a national travel agent trade association.

TRAVEL AGENCIES

A *travel agency* is a retailer who has the authority to sell travel services to consumers on behalf of certain travel suppliers (such as airlines, cruise lines, and car rental companies). Under contract laws, the travel retailer is the *agent*, while the travel supplier is the *principal*. Other than basic contract laws, there are few state or federal laws or regulations governing the operations of travel agents.

In the mid-1990's, the major U.S. airlines began cutting the commissions paid to travel agents for selling airline tickets, from a standard level of 10% to zero. As a result, many travel agencies began charging service fees to travelers, raising questions about whether they represent the interests of travel suppliers or their traveling clients. The courts have now begun holding travel agents in some cases to a higher standard of care for consumers, as the relationship between travel suppliers and agents has continued to evolve. Also, travel agents will more likely be held responsible if they caused the problem in your trip (for example, making an incorrect reservation) than if they had no direct control over the problem (for example, recommending the car rental company that owns the vehicle in which you were injured in a traffic accident).

Therefore, though travel agents continue to owe you the usual duties and responsibilities that any retail salesperson owes to a customer, some aspects of the law are changing to hold the agent more accountable to consumers. The degree of responsibility for agents depends largely on two factors:

1. whether you have paid service fees directly to the travel agent, with the assumption that the agent is therefore working in your best interests and
2. whether the agent is simply making reservations on your behalf or providing professional travel counseling services and packaging your trip.

The more involved your agent is in choosing suppliers and making final decisions on trip components, and the more money the agent earns from suppliers (for steering business their way) or from you (for professional advice), the more likely it is that the agency may be held liable if something goes wrong with your trip.

A third (albeit minor) factor is the degree of disclosure on the part of the agent. As long as the agent tells you specifically which suppliers are involved in your trip (that is, the names of the airlines, cruise lines, hotels, and other companies), then the agent is considered to be working for *disclosed principals*. If the agent did not deliberately deceive you in some way, then the principals (the suppliers) bear primary liability for your trip. However, if the travel agent arranged a trip for you without disclosing the principals, so that you assumed that the agent was packaging the trip from scratch, then the agent assumes some of the liability of the principals. In this case, you may seek damages from both the agent and the suppliers. Regardless of the shift from suppliers to customers, travel agents typically perform three basic types of services.

Providing Professional Travel Recommendations

Travel agents stay updated on the latest information about travel suppliers, destinations, travel conditions, and other industry news from many different sources. These sources include supplier brochures, newsletters, and websites; travel trade magazines and newspapers; consumer travel media; feedback from their clients; their own personal travel experiences; and, word-of-mouth reports. Professional agents use this information—combined with their practical work experience in selling travel—to give consumers appraisals and recommendations on specific destinations and suppliers. In fact, travel agents have a duty to exercise reasonable care in learning about travel industry news so that they can advise consumers properly to avoid unnecessary travel risks.

However, this duty is limited, and agents are not required to conduct background checks or investigations on suppliers. The most important data they must monitor are the reputation, track record, and financial condition of major travel suppliers. If travel agents have heard or read about problems with a particular company or they have received complaints from past clients about the company, they must pass along that information to you if the information would likely affect your decision to use the supplier.

In recent years, travelers have successfully sued agents who did not tell them about substandard conditions or construction delays at hotels, an airline's impending bankruptcy, the common risks that occur when an airline defaults, and complaints about a tour operator.

The liability of travel agents may turn on the question of whether it is reasonable to assume that they should have known about or anticipated a problem with your trip. If a cruise line's financial troubles have been widely reported in major travel trade publications, but your travel agent books you a cabin with that company anyway, you should have a strong case for negligence if the cruise line defaults or ceases operations. Sometimes, however, travel suppliers, such as tour operators, literally shut their doors and turn off their phones overnight, leaving travelers stranded on trips around the globe. In those cases, it may be much tougher to argue that your travel agent should have expected this shutdown to occur.

Another critical factor in assessing the agent's liability is your level of involvement in planning the trip. If you insist that your travel agent book you with a specific travel company, even after the agent warns you about potential problems, then it is not likely that the agent would be held responsible for any ensuing problems on your trip.

Visa

It is not clear whether your travel agent has an obligation to advise you about visas and other requirements for entering another country. While many countries in Europe that are popular tourist destinations for Americans now participate in the U.S. Visa Waiver Program (see p.159), many other nations still require U.S. travelers to obtain a visa prior to entering their borders. These visas are generally available at each country's U.S. embassy or consulates. If you arrive at one of these destinations without the required visa (or other paperwork, such as immunization records), you will likely be denied entry by the country's immigration officials and sent home. In fact, it is likely that the airline will not let you board the airplane without the required documents for entering the country to which you are flying.

In the past, it was assumed that travelers were primarily responsible for learning about the legal requirements of traveling abroad. However, in at least one court case, the travel agent was ruled negligent for failing to tell a client about the visa requirement.

Travel Risks

Generally, if the travel agent knows about a substantial travel risk to the client (such as a tour operator that is threatening to shut down), the agent must warn the client about this risk. There are three significant exceptions to this rule.

> 1. Travel agents do not have to point out or explain the fine print in any agreements between travel suppliers and you (although many helpful agents will try to answer your questions about these details). If a cruise line's brochure or passenger contract limits the

company's liability, requires a specific venue for legal disagreements, or restricts your rights in other ways, it is your responsibility to learn about and understand these terms and conditions. The travel agent is not required to act as your attorney. Therefore, you should always insist on seeing the fine print from any supplier that might affect your trip.

2. Travel agents do not have to warn you about any risks that would be obviously apparent to anyone.

3. Travel agents do not have to predict the future for you. In other words, they cannot be held responsible in most instances for factors that are totally out of their control, such as natural disasters, surprise strikes, or inclement weather. For example, travel agents are not required to warn travelers that it might rain during their vacation or that the roads leading to a popular ski resort might be blocked by snow.

As a general practice, many agents will pass along to their clients any government travel warnings, such as U.S. State Department travel advisories that have been issued about potentially dangerous areas of the world. For example, the *World Health Organization*, the *U.S. Centers for Disease Control and Prevention*, and the State Department issued alerts for travelers considering trips to Hong Kong, Canada (Toronto), and other destinations after the outbreak of the Severe Acute Respiratory Syndrome (SARS) virus in 2003. In this instance, most travel agents advised their clients who had booked trips to these areas that federal and global officials were recommending avoiding these destinations until the SARS virus was controlled.

Professional travel agents monitor these agencies' announcements directly or they receive notice of new announcements from their trade associations. Depending on the severity of the announcement—a travel alert or advisory with general advice about potential travel hazards or a travel warning with specific instructions to avoid or leave a specific destination—your travel agent may contact you directly via mail, phone, fax, or email with the details of the announcement. If you encounter danger while traveling and you learn later that a respected federal or global agency had issued a travel warning before you left on your trip, then you may have a reasonable claim against your travel agent for failing to communicate this news to you prior to departure.

Injuries

Sometimes, travelers will bring claims against travel agents because they were injured while traveling. Courts rarely hold agents responsible for such injuries. Obvious hazards over which agents have no direct control are generally outside any liability that can be imposed on the agent.

Crimes

Unless the travel agent knows (or should know) about high levels of criminal activity in a particular destination, the courts have ruled that agents cannot be held responsible for crimes committed over which they have no control and could not have reasonably foreseen.

Health and Safety Risks

Finally, one area in which the courts have begun holding travel agents to a higher standard of disclosure is health and safety risks in other countries. In a number of recent cases, judges have concluded that agents stand in a better position to know about required immunizations, medical precautions, government travel advisories and warnings, and other signs of trouble. Therefore, the agents should be held responsible for disclosing such information to their clients.

You should make it a practice to ask your travel agent specifically about any health and safety risks or warnings in effect for your proposed trip. You can also confirm the agent's advisories at the websites of the *U.S. Centers for Disease Control and Prevention* at **www.cdc.gov/travel** and the State Department at **http:// travel.state.gov**.

Making and Confirming Reservations with Travel Suppliers

After travel agents have given their professional advice on the destinations and other details for a given trip, they will contact the desired travel suppliers—usually via their *computerized reservations systems* (CRS's), the desktop terminals that connect them with supplier inventories, but sometimes via phone or fax or even regular mail—to determine the availability of accommodations, tickets, or other services for the chosen date and time of travel and to confirm the specific terms of the reservations (time, price, number of travelers, restrictions, etc.).

Your agent is required to make the very best good-faith effort to follow your directions completely in making your reservations. If the agent fails to make the reservations properly and you are injured or suffer any loss as a result, you may successfully argue that the agent should be held responsible. For example, if you find an ad in the local newspaper for a deeply discounted airfare that must be booked within the next seven days and you call your travel agent immediately to request the booking, your travel agent might be liable if she forgets to book that flight for you and the deadline for the discounted fare passes.

Note: *The agent would be responsible only for errors within his or her control. If he or she contacts the airline for you while you are on the phone with him or her, and the airline says that the discounted flight is sold out, the agent cannot be judged liable because the discounted seats sold so quickly.*

The most common travel agent errors involve booking mistakes. For example, you asked for a hotel room in San Juan, Puerto Rico, but the agent confirms a room for you in San Juan, Texas. Or you arrive at the rental car counter to find that your confirmed reservation is for a standard car, not the minivan you specifically requested. If you can show that there is a material difference (in terms of cost, geography, etc.) between what you asked for and what you received, the agent should be held responsible for making up that difference.

Travel agents are generally responsible for making any confirmations required by travel suppliers for your reservations. When travel agents book their clients with tour operators or other types of trip packagers (such as charter companies for popular sporting events), they may be held liable for not confirming your reservations directly with the travel suppliers involved in the tour package. Reputable travel agents carry professional liability/errors and omissions insurance to protect them against losses from these types of mistakes.

Issuing Tickets and Collecting Payments for Suppliers

After your reservations have been made, the travel agent provides you with the actual tickets, vouchers, receipts, and other tangible proof of your reservations. In some cases, the agent may arrange with the travel supplier to send you these documents, directly.

If the issued ticket contains an error such as the incorrect fare or a wrong date, the travel agent should take all reasonable steps to correct the error. However, simple errors are different than changes made by travel suppliers (such as drops in fares) after your ticket has been issued. An example would be if you book a cruise through a travel agent who then sends you the cruise line's boarding documents and the cruise line then drops its pricing at the last minute to fill remaining empty cabins on the ship. Your travel agent is not generally required to check the cruise line's fares continuously and re-ticket you at the lower fare (though many professional agents will indeed alert you if cruise lines drop their prices).

In the end, the travel agent is rarely judged to be responsible for your enjoyment of the trip. The agent becomes liable only when there is some proof that he or she was negligent and at fault in arranging your trip properly.

CONSOLIDATORS

Unlike travel agencies or travel websites that simply act as retailers processing sales for the airlines, consolidators are companies that purchase airline capacity at a bulk price for reselling to travel agencies and the general public. The airlines rely on consolidators to market *distressed inventory*, especially unfilled seats on overseas flights. Though the effects of September 11 and the rise of deeply discounted Web airfares have driven smaller consolidators out of business, the surviving companies have expanded beyond distressed tickets to offer more standard seats (and, today, more tickets for U.S. domestic flights) on a wholesale basis.

Many savvy travel agents have saved their clients hundreds of dollars on international flights by purchasing the tickets through a consolidator. Generally, the consolidator offers a net fare to the agent—at savings ranging from 20% to as much as 80% off the standard published airfare—who then marks up the ticket before selling it to the traveler. Even with the agent's markup, consolidator fares represent a substantial savings over the prices offered directly by the airlines.

Some consolidators also sell directly to the public as well as travel agencies. More consolidators today also offer tour packages built around their discounted airline tickets. While consolidator tickets have traditionally been popular with leisure travelers, some companies now report a growing number of corporate travelers using their tickets for international business trips.

In exchange for the savings, however, consolidator tickets typically carry significant restrictions on their use. For example, they may be valid only for certain travel dates, may not qualify for frequent flier miles, or may be completely nonrefundable.

Always ask your travel agent or consolidator for a written explanation of the restrictions on a consolidator ticket and review these terms thoroughly before you purchase the ticket to ensure that you understand them. Because consolidator tickets do carry such restrictions, your travel agent may require you to sign a disclaimer stating that you were told about them. Also, you should investigate how long the consolidator has been in business, whether the company's ownership has changed recently, and how often your travel agent recommends the company to other travelers.

Finally, never pay for a consolidator ticket with a check or cash. You should always insist on using your credit card. Consolidators sometimes close their doors without warning. Because you have not purchased your ticket directly from the airline, it is not unusual for travelers to pay for a consolidator ticket that they never receive. If you bought the ticket using your credit card, you can request a charge back from the issuing bank.

(Consolidators have sprung up in the cruise and hotel fields now, but most companies focus primarily on selling airline tickets.)

TRAVEL WEBSITES

The world of travel turned upside down in the late 1990s with the explosive growth in Internet sites devoted to the selling of travel. Seventy percent of U.S. travelers now use the Internet to research travel options and prices. Billions and billions are spent on Web-based travel reservations. Currently, those sales represent a very small percentage of the travel industry's total sales, but experts predict that the market share of online travel sites will continue to expand steadily. Many of these sites offer *Web-only* fares and discounts, as well as exclusive benefits such as frequent flier mile bonuses for purchases. Today, travel is the largest segment of e-commerce, totaling more sales than books, music, or any other good or service sold via the Internet.

Two primary types of travel websites have emerged. *Bookable* sites are those offered by individual airlines, cruise lines, or other travel suppliers for consumers to make reservations directly with the company. Many brick and mortar travel agencies now have their own bookable websites as well for clients to use. *Internet travel agencies* are sites that allow travelers to search the inventory of competing travel suppliers before booking their trip.

Generally, travel websites carry the same responsibilities and fall under the same requirements and regulations as traditional travel agencies. Because they do not have a physical business location where the great majority of their customers live, however, these sites pose new challenges for consumers.

Most states have laws that give their courts jurisdiction over companies that conduct business with their citizens despite having a minimal physical presence inside the state. Factors in determining whether a company falls under a state's jurisdiction include the reasonableness of the state's claim of jurisdiction, the extent to which a company conducts business within the state, and how the claims being made relate to the company's in-state business activities.

Under these jurisdiction rules, travel websites will generally be governed by the courts in your state if they are interactive. In other words, if they request information from you or if they allow you to make online reservations and pay for them. Passive websites (travel suppliers' *online brochures* that do not accept emails or allow online reservations or payments) may not fall under the state's jurisdiction.

Many travel websites now have *forum selection clauses* buried in the fine print of their online contracts. If you use the site to book and pay for a travel service, you automatically agree (as part of the contract) that you will bring any legal actions against the company in its home state or another jurisdiction outside your home state. Many courts uphold these clauses, as long as you have had the chance to read the fine print on the website.

The fine print in the *terms and conditions* statement of many travel websites (usually found via a tiny link on the home page) also contains other hidden dangers for consumers. For example, a *Travel Weekly* study of the websites of the seven largest U.S. airlines (*American, United, Delta, Continental, Northwest, Southwest,* and *US Airways*), as well as *Orbitz, Expedia,* and *Travelocity,* discovered that these sites provide all fare quotes and reservations *as is.* This means you have no remedy if the information shown on a site is incorrect or if the site makes a mistake in finalizing your booking.

Further, these sites disclaim all warranties of suitability for a particular purpose, meaning the site's owners have no responsibility if the site does not work as expected. All of the sites except *Delta.com* and *Southwest.com* require you to waive all claims for money damages.

To protect your rights when you use a travel website, always look at the site as if it were a brick and mortar travel company. See whether the site posts its industry affiliations or any seals of approval from the *Better Business Bureau* and other consumer protection agencies (as well as required state seller of travel license or registration numbers). Steer clear of any travel site that does not list a physical address and phone number.

Read the site's terms and conditions and its privacy statement. Always use your credit card (never your debit card) so that you may request a *charge back* from the issuing bank if the website does not deliver as promised. Also, never use your credit card on a site that does not transmit data using secure servers.

Always keep a paper trail—including printouts of confirmations, itineraries, and purchase agreements—so that you have a record of your transactions. It also pays to contact the travel suppliers (the airline, hotel, cruise line, etc., with which you are booked) directly to confirm your reservation. For example, many hotel discount websites take consumer reservations via email or online forms, but they transmit the request to the individual hotels via faxes. It is not unusual for consumers who have purchased hotel rooms over the Internet to show up at a hotel front desk where the clerk has no record of your reservation, even though you have the travel website's printout in your hands.

Finally, keep in mind when you book over the Internet that many leading online travel agencies accept incentive payments from airlines and other suppliers, leading to what some observers have called *display bias*. This happens when the screen shows travel options for you based not on price or the other selection criteria you have picked, but rather on the placement of *preferred* vendors at the top of the screen.

STATE-SPECIFIC LAWS

Several states have enacted *seller of travel* or *travel promoter* laws to regulate travel sales in their jurisdictions and to protect consumers when travel suppliers or agents go out of business or defraud travelers. If you reside in one of the following states, and you have problems dealing with a travel agent or supplier located in your state, contact the state attorney general's office immediately to ask whether the agent or supplier violated the seller of travel statute.

California

The state of California enforces the toughest seller of travel law in the nation. The state requires registration by both travel agents with a California business address and out-of-state agents that sell to California residents or advertise within the state (including websites). Currently, more than 6,000 travel agencies have registered with the state attorney general's office. In addition, registered agencies (whether they sell wholesale or retail) must maintain a trust account if they sell any air or sea travel (sellers of land-only packages are exempted). As an alternative, agencies may substitute a bond for the trust account in an amount equal to what would be held in the trust account.

In-state agencies registered in California must also contribute annually to a restitution fund to reimburse California consumers due to bankruptcy, insolvency, cessation of operations or material failure of any registered in-state agency. Under state law, the fund must be maintained at a minimum of $1.6 million (currently, the fund has $2.9 million).

Also, registered agencies (in-state and out-of-state) must disclose to consumers the following information in writing:
- the total trip cost;
- payment schedule;
- names of suppliers;
- departure details;
- all terms and conditions including cancellation conditions;

- the consumer's refund rights; and,
- a statement about the agency's trust account, its contributions to the restitution fund and/or any alternative provisions it makes to protect consumer funds and the details of consumer's right to make claims on these protections. In circumstances when a consumer cannot make a claim on the fund, agencies must disclose that orally and in writing.

Registered agencies must display their current registration certificates so that they are easily visible to the public, They must display their registration numbers conspicuously on all advertising and promotional materials delivered in any manner—including their websites.

Florida

The state of Florida requires travel agencies—firms that have a business location in Florida as well as out-of-state firms that sell to Florida residents—to register and obtain a bond of up to $25,000 (or up to $50,000, if the agency sells travel certificates) or provide an alternative surety such as a letter of credit. Agencies accredited by the *Airlines Reporting Corporation* (ARC) are exempt from registering and bonding if they have had the same owners for three years (five years if selling travel certificates). In addition, the state may waive the bond rule for any travel seller with at least five years of experience selling travel in Florida in good standing. Common carriers (such as airlines and cruise lines) and providers of accommodations (such as hotels and bed and breakfasts) are excluded.

Registered agencies must display their certificates prominently at their primary place of business. They must list their registration number on all contracts of sale and advertisements.

Hawaii

The state of Hawaii requires travel agencies located within the state to register and to maintain trust accounts. In addition to these rules, charter tour operators must also maintain bonds. Registered agencies must provide written disclosure regarding trips as follows: prices and payment-due dates, trip details, names of suppliers, cancellation and other terms, details on the agency's trust account, and information on consumer rights. These disclosure forms must be approved by the state before they are used.

If some contracted travel services were not provided, consumers have the right to a refund within fourteen days of requesting it, less any cancellation fees and any amounts held by travel suppliers.

Illinois

The state of Illinois imposes rules on *travel promoters*, defined as companies that do not have *Airlines Reporting Corporation* (ARC) approval or do not have $1 million in errors and omission insurance plus a $100,000 bond. Travel promoters must maintain a trust account for clients' funds, but the state does not require actual registration. They must also disclose the following information to consumers:

- pricing;
- name of supplier of transportation and other specifics;
- cancellation terms;
- location and bank number of the trust account; and,
- details of the customer's right to a refund if transportation is canceled through no fault of the customer.

The promoter cannot advertise air or sea transportation unless it has contracted for that transportation.

Iowa

The state of Iowa requires in-state and out-of-state travel agencies to register if they do business with travelers in Iowa. Non-Airline Reporting Corporation agencies must post a $10,000 bond or provide an alternative surety, such as a letter of credit.

Massachusetts

The commonwealth of Massachusetts requires travel agents, tour operators, cruise lines, charter tour operators, travel club operators, and travel certificate sellers to disclose—usually orally and in writing—details on each supplier, price, payment due dates, trip details, terms of any substitution policy, terms of any cancellation or refund policy, and terms of any cancellation insurance (including its limitations). Also, these companies must disclose any facts that might influence a consumer not to buy the travel service.

Once a sale has occurred, the agency must advise the consumer when and how each payment will be made to suppliers and provide a written confirmation within five days after each payment was made, as well as written confirmation within two days after any reservation has been made. If the agency violates these rules, the consumer has the right to cancel and must receive a refund within thirty days. (All of the mentioned rules do not apply to services provided to business travelers.)

Also, if a seller acting as a tour operator fails to provide what is promised, it must give the customer the option of a refund or substitute services and refund the difference if the new service is lower in standards.

Nevada

The state of Nevada requires travel agencies to register. Non-Airlines Reporting Corporation agencies must also post a $50,000 bond or provide an alternative surety such as a letter of credit. Exempted are transportation companies when their business is limited to providing transportation, as well as hotels when they plan services for their own guests.

Registered agencies must display their certificates so that they are easily visible to the public.

Ohio

The state of Ohio requires travel agents and tour promoters (sellers of travel without approval from Airlines Reporting Corporation or the International Airline Travel Agents Network) to register with the state. Agencies and promoters that sell only intrastate travel must post a $20,000 bond. Registered agencies must display their number and the words "Registered Ohio Travel Agency" or "Registered Ohio Tour Promoter" in all advertising within the state.

Rhode Island

The state of Rhode Island targets in-state agencies only with its law. These agents must obtain licenses from the state and post $10,000 bonds. Travel agency managers and individual agents are also tested and licensed. In addition, agents must disclose a range of information to their customers: pricing details, name of carrier and transportation specifics, conditions of sale including cancellation terms, and all parties' rights and obligations depending on the reason for cancellation. Also, agents are required to advise of changes to any travel paid for and of changes in accommodations, with a refund for any appropriate difference if the quality is lower than what was purchased. If the agency breaches its duty of care, it must refund the customer's payments within forty-five days.

Registered agents and agencies must post their licenses conspicuously in their places of business. The agency's registration number must appear in all advertising. These ads must also show prices for promoted products and tell which components are included in the posted prices. Additionally, agency ads must indicate when a promoted airfare is only one-way and what kind of role any tour guides will play in the promoted trip.

Washington

The state of Washington requires travel agencies to register and to maintain trust accounts or provide an alternative surety, such as a bond ranging from $10,000 to $50,000, depending on the agency's sales volume. *Airlines Reporting Corporation* agencies are exempted from having the trust account or bond, and other agencies may seek exemption if their owners swear that they never hold customers' funds more than five days. Registered agencies must disclose, in eight-point boldface type, information such as the amounts paid and payment due dates, supplier names, all known trip details (with full information to be provided with final documents), the details of cancellation penalties, and the agency's registration number. The law also provides a schedule for refunding money due to customers after a cancellation by any party.

Registration numbers must be posted conspicuously in the place of business and must appear in advertising that includes products with prices or dates. Also, agencies are forbidden to advertise products unless they know they are available when the ad was placed. The seller of travel is expected to keep written or printed documentation of the steps taken to verify that the advertised offer was available at the time the advertising was placed and to keep those records for a year.

chapter eight:
Travel Finance and Insurance

Since the days when *American Express* introduced the slogan "Don't Leave Home Without It," travelers have grown conditioned to expect the worst when it comes to handling their money on the road. They face two primary challenges that threaten their bank accounts (and their peace of mind):

1. *nickel and dime fees*, hidden charges, and unanticipated expenses that add up considerably by the end of the trip and
2. major unexpected delays, serious illnesses or injuries, travel supplier defaults or bankruptcies, or other catastrophes that ruin the trip and waste hundreds or thousands of dollars in the process.

This chapter highlights the primary finance and insurance pitfalls for travelers, along with solutions to prevent these clouds from raining down on your trip.

CREDIT AND DEBIT CARDS

The average American consumer carries at least three major credit cards. Bank debit cards have grown in popularity since the late 1990s. Whether you are traveling on business or pleasure, these cards are a handy, convenient, and a safe means of paying for trip expenses without the risks of carrying large amounts of cash. However, many consumers worry about the threat of identity theft, credit card fraud, hidden billing charges, and other issues that come with using these cards.

Federal law limits your responsibility for unauthorized charges to $50. However, preventing a problem is always better than dealing with one. Follow these tips when using credit cards or debit cards when you travel.

- Carry only those cards that you absolutely plan to use on your trip.
- Keep the cards stored in your purse or wallet, not loose in your pockets.
- In your suitcase or another safe place, store a list of your card account numbers and the correct telephone numbers for reporting lost or stolen cards. Consider signing up with a service (offered by many banks and AAA branches) to notify all of your card issuers with a single phone call if your cards are lost or stolen.
- After you use the card for a purchase, make sure that the card is returned to you. Keep any carbon receipts or watch them as they are destroyed. Check the sales receipts for accuracy and make sure that the areas on the charge slip for the numerals and decimal points are filled in.
- Never write your card number on a check.
- Keep all ATM receipts, rather than throwing them away.

Travel Tip

Copying credit cards is a growing scam, especially in Europe and Latin America. Consider paying at the register (even in restaurants) rather than handing over your card.

Charge backs

Purchasing travel goods and services with a credit card gives you one very important safeguard—the right to request a *charge back*. This is a reversal of the charge placed on your account.

Example:

If you book a cruise using your credit card and the cruise line ceases operations before you take the trip, contact your issuing bank and ask that the price of the cruise be refunded to your account.

Keep in mind, though, that federal regulations governing charge backs include several important limitations.

Traveling on Business

If you use your corporate credit card or your personal credit card while you are traveling on business, you may not be allowed to request charge backs. Federal charge back rules protect only *natural persons*, meaning that businesses and corporations do not technically qualify. These rules do not apply to extensions of credit primarily for business purposes. However, some issuing banks and credit card companies waive these exceptions as part of their cardholder agreements, meaning that they accept charge back requests for business travel regardless of the federal standards. Ask your bank or card issuer for its policies.

Debit Cards

Debit cards do not operate as credit cards and therefore these federal rules do not apply to travel purchases made with debit cards. Even though some banks have standard policies allowing you to contest a debit card transaction if you did not receive the service as promised, you should rarely use your debit card for major travel purchases such as trip

Travel Tip

When you purchase any item outside the U.S. that the shop will box or bag for you, check inside before you leave the shop to make sure it is the same item you ordered. Unscrupulous stores will switch cheaper items that you may not discover until you have returned home.

deposits. (Reserve them instead for buying film, small souvenirs, personal toiletries, etc.)

Time Limitations

Federal rules limit charge backs to purchases made within 100 miles of your home or made with a merchant located anywhere as long as you file a claim within sixty days after the first bill containing the questionable transaction was mailed to you. The credit card company must acknowledge your complaint in writing within thirty days after receiving it (unless the problem has been resolved). The company must resolve the complaint within two billing cycles (but not more than ninety days) after receiving your claim.

On the surface, these regulations might apparently prevent you from charging back any trip deposits or payments, since you may pay the travel supplier located in another state or country many months before the departure. However, major credit card companies have loosened their own policies for travel charge backs, giving you as long as nine months after the billing date to file a claim. If you encounter a problem, contact your card company or issuing bank and ask for a representative who handles travel-related complaints.

Travel Tip

If you plan to change a large amount of currency, check exchange rates at your hotel or at an independent currency exchange before withdrawing local currency from an ATM with your credit or debit card. The bank charges will usually prove much higher than the hotel's fees.

Foreign Exchange Conversion Fees

Beware of any *foreign exchange conversion fees* that your credit card company may charge cardholders when they use their cards to make purchases outside the United States. *Visa* and *MasterCard* charge issuing banks a 1% fee on these transactions, which the banks typically pass along to consumers.

In addition, many banks, such as *J.P. Morgan Chase*, *Citibank*, and *Bank One*, add an additional 2%. The notable exception is *MBNA Corp.*, which does not add its own fees to the *Visa* and *MasterCard* charges.

American Express charges as much as 2% above the actual amount of any overseas transaction. However, in 2003, a California state court ruled that *Visa* and *MasterCard might* be forced to refund these fees in many cases because cardholders did not receive adequate notice of the added charges.

VALUE ADDED TAXES

Canada and many European countries charge *value added taxes* (VAT), a type of federal sales tax on purchases that can run as much as 20% of the price tag. The United States has no federal sales tax or VAT, though almost all states and some cities charge sales taxes of their own. As a U.S. traveler, you may qualify for a refund of the VAT on your international purchases.

Canada

In Canada, the federal *Goods and Services Tax* (GST) is 7% and almost every Canadian province also assesses a *Provincial Sales Tax* (PST). You may claim a refund of the GST paid on items taken out of Canada within sixty days of purchase and on hotel room rentals. However, Canada does not permit GST refunds on tobacco, alcoholic beverages, meals, car rentals, and fuel.

You must fill out the GST refund forms distributed by many stores and hotels. You, then, must submit the form with your original receipts attached. Each receipt submitted for a refund must be at least Can $50 (in other words, you cannot add five receipts for Can $10 each to qualify). The minimum GST refund is Can $7. You must file your claim within one year of any included purchase. You may file only one refund request per calendar year quarter.

If your claimed purchases total less than Can $500, you may file your claim at the airport or the border station. Otherwise, you can mail your claim to Canadian authorities. To ask for a PST refund, check with each province for its specific requirements. (Always file your GST refund request first, as some provinces are notorious for not returning your receipts.)

Europe

In Europe, you may file a VAT refund request on the spot when you make a purchase in a store, but the rules vary greatly from store to store. Other options include VAT refund counters at airports or using a service such as Global Refund that will process your request for an average commission of 3%. Check with your travel agent or with the stores in which you buy items for additional details.

VAT refunds from European countries may take months to process, but do not minimize the importance of filing a request, as the VAT usually apply to everything from a cup of coffee to a designer gown. The rates run from 13.8% in Germany and Spain to 20% in Denmark and Sweden.

BUSINESS TRAVEL TAX RULES

When you travel for business purposes, you can generally deduct your travel expenses if you incur the expenses for a legitimate business reason, if you do not receive reimbursements, *per diem* expense allowances, or other compensation for those expenses.

You must declare these expenses as itemized deductions on IRS Form 2106 attached to your IRS Form 1040 if you are an employee. Use Schedule C if you are self-employed; Schedule F if you

Travel Tip

Taxi meters in the U.S. and abroad are sometimes rigged. Always ask a local person or your hotel what the taxi ride should cost. Settle on a price with the driver before you get into the car.

are a farmer; or, Schedule E if you earn royalties. Your travel deductions will be limited to the amount that exceeds 2% of your adjusted gross income. To be eligible for deductions, your travel expenses must be incurred while you are away from your *tax home* (your main place of business) longer than an average day.

Deductible Expenses

Deductible business expenses are those typical (but necessary) expenses you incur when you travel away from your home.

- **Transportation.**

  You can usually deduct the cost of airline, rail, and bus tickets between your tax home and your business destination. (Do not forget to request and keep your receipts for taxis, shuttle vans, and other transportation expenses. Frequent Flier tickets do not count.) Also, you may deduct transportation expenses between the airport, railway station, or bus terminal and your hotel, as well as the hotel and any meeting places, clients' offices, or similar work locations.

- **Auto expenses.**

  You may deduct the cost of renting a car for a business trip. If you use a car that you own instead, you may deduct actual business-related, car expenses (such as gas receipts for a business trip) or the standard IRS mileage rate.

- **Lodging.**

  You can deduct the cost of your hotel room if your business trip lasts overnight (or at least long enough so that you must rest or sleep before you return home).

- **Meals.**

  You can deduct the cost of meals only if the business trip lasts overnight. Otherwise, you may not deduct meals on shorter trips. Your deduction is limited to 50% of what you spend on food, beverage, taxes, and tips.

You cannot deduct meals that would be considered extravagant.

- **Incidental expenses.**
  You may deduct the cost of business telephone calls, faxes, and Internet connections while you are traveling away from home on business. You can also deduct reasonable laundry and cleaning expenses, but not if you take the standard meal allowance described in IRS Publication 463. That allowance actually covers both food and incidental expenses.

- **Entertainment expenses.**
  The general rule of thumb is that you can deduct only 50% of your business entertainment expenses.

- **Expenses for other travelers.**
  If you are traveling with other individuals who are your employees with a genuine reason for accompanying you on business, you may pay for their travel expenses and deduct them as if they were your own.

You cannot deduct expenses for your spouse, other family members, or friends who travel with you unless they meet this standard.

Possible Deductions

If you attend a convention or conference, you can generally deduct the related travel expenses if you can demonstrate that the event helps your business directly. However, you may not deduct travel expenses for your spouse or family members who accompany you, unless they are actively involved in your busi-

---

Travel Tip

In order to maintain low-cost cell phone calls overseas, buy a local Subscriber Identity Module calling card for the country you are visiting. For more details, check:

www.telestial.com

www.ustronics.com

www.buyundercost.com

ness. Unrelated expenses, such as sightseeing tours or social fees, are not deductible.

Conventions held outside North America pose a special challenge, as you may be required to show that the conference is directly related to your business and that it was just as reasonable to hold the event outside North America as inside it. (The purpose of these rules is to prevent business people from claiming vacations as business trips.)

If you take a cruise for business purposes, you may not claim these expenses as a deduction unless the ship is registered in the United States and the stops on the itinerary are U.S. ports. Your deduction will be capped at twice the federal per diem rate—the maximum daily travel expenses allowed for federal employees as found in IRS Publication 463— in effect at the time of the cruise. For any given year, you will be limited to $2,000 in deductions for travel expenses related to cruise meetings.

> **Travel Tip**
>
> When you travel for business reasons, keep original receipts and records of your costs, as well as any per diem advances or reimbursements you receive for those costs. Your receipts must conform to the standards explained in IRS Publication 463.

CHARITY TRAVEL TAX RULES

If you travel on behalf of a tax-exempt organization such as your church, a nonprofit foundation, or a similar charity, your travel expenses may qualify as a charitable contribution. You may be allowed to deduct those expenses from your taxes. This contribution must be voluntary on your part. You must offer it without expecting to receive any tangible benefits of equal value in return. You will record such deductions as charitable contributions on Schedule A of IRS Form 1040. (For complete details concerning charitable contributions, check IRS Publication 526. You can print the information from the Internet by going to **www.irs.gov**.)

The IRS will allow you to claim a charitable contribution deduction for travel expenses as long as you spend most of the time during your trip performing work for the charity (instead of your own personal recreation). You may deduct all reasonable travel expenses, including air/rail/bus tickets, car expenses, taxi fares or airport shuttles, lodging costs, and meal costs.

Unlike business travel deductions, there is no standard meal allowance when traveling for a charity. You can deduct the entire cost of the meal. If the charity gives you a *per diem* travel allowance and the allowance does not cover all of your travel costs, then you may deduct the difference as a charitable contribution.

Note: *If the per diem exceeds your actual travel expenses and you do not return the difference to the charity, then you must declare the difference as income.*

Regarding conventions, you may deduct your actual travel expenses if you attend the event as an authorized representative or delegate of the charitable organization. For your records, you should obtain a letter from the charity stating that you have been chosen to represent this group at the conference. In no instance can you deduct personal expenses for entertainment such as theater tickets or sightseeing tours or the expenses of your spouse, children, or other persons. As with business travel, you should keep as many of your original receipts as possible.

Note: *U.S. tax regulations change frequently with little notice. Applying the rules for business and charity travel deductions can be a tricky process. Always consult your tax professional for advice before you apply the suggestions contained in this chapter.*

TRAVEL INSURANCE

Since September 11, many travel insurance companies have reported double and triple digit sales increases as more consumers worry about their potential expenses and liabilities if something goes wrong on their trip. While some types of travel insurance coverage may be helpful in certain circumstances, many provisions in these policies may duplicate your existing insurance protection in automobile, homeowners, and business or personal liability policies. To avoid wasting money, you should understand what specific types of insurance you will need while on the road to fill in those gaps. Only purchase the coverage that you absolutely need.

> **Travel Tip**
>
> Some travel insurers will add your minor children who are traveling with you to your policy at no extra charge. Ask your travel agent or insurance company about this discount.

The first step in this process is determining the levels, limits, and restrictions in your existing insurance policies.

- Your life insurance policy usually covers accidental death and dismemberment, even when you are traveling outside your home state.
- Your homeowners' or renter's policy may include liability, baggage, or personal property protection while you are on the road.
- Your health insurance policy may provide a minimal level of coverage when you travel (but many policies, such as Medicare, exclude treatment if you are traveling outside the United States).
- Your automobile insurance may include coverage for rental cars.
- Your credit cards may offer minimal amounts of insurance protection, including flight insurance and rental car coverage.

Secondary Insurance

Keep in mind that many travel insurance policies provide *secondary* or *excess* coverage, meaning that your other forms of insurance protection (including your existing life, homeowners', automobile, and health coverage) will be tapped before the travel insurance. Also, be aware that travel insurance policies generally contain a large number of *exclusion* clauses that negate your coverage and that typically lie hidden until you actually attempt to file a claim.

Third Party Coverage

Next, you should confirm that the travel insurance you plan to purchase is *third party coverage* underwritten by an independent insurance company (and not the travel supplier or travel agent who is selling you the coverage). Many cruise lines and tour operators earn excellent profits by packaging and selling insurance policies to their passengers. However, these supplier-underwritten policies are rarely a safe investment, in that the coverage generally ceases to exist if the cruise line or tour operator ceases operations or declares bankruptcy.

Permission to Cancel

Suppliers also sell plans called *cancellation penalty waivers* or *cancel for any reason policies*. These waivers are not technically insurance, but rather the company's permission for you to cancel the trip without being assessed cancellation penalties. These waivers typically expire several days before your trip starts (the time when many last-minute crises arise) and have many hidden exclusions. The average travel insurance policy provides much greater protection against cancellation risks for less money. These waivers are designed to repay consumers with future travel credits only, whereas standard travel insurance policies cover claims with cash.

> ### Travel Tip
>
> Ask your travel agent to explain—in detail and in writing—how your policy is underwritten and why you should purchase the policy he or she recommends. You need to make an informed purchase.

Types of Cancellation Insurance

The most important component of any comprehensive travel insurance policy is coverage for expenses and liabilities if a trip is cancelled or interrupted. Your existing types of personal insurance generally do not cover these risks.

Trip Cancellation Insurance

This type of insurance protects you before the trip starts, reimbursing you for any prepaid travel expenses that cannot be refunded (such as cruise deposits and airline tickets) if you must cancel the trip. Every policy has different clauses, but in general terms, this coverage is triggered when three factors occur:

1. you must cancel your prearranged, prepaid trip;
2. you must cancel for a reason that you could not have anticipated or prevented; and,
3. the reason for canceling affects your family, a traveling companion, your business partner, or you personally.

Commonly covered reasons include:
- supplier default;
- the illness or death of a family member or traveling companion;
- any labor disputes;
- natural disasters or weather conditions that interrupt travel services for more than a day; and,
- the unexpected termination of your employment.

When you consider purchasing trip cancellation coverage, make sure that the coverage begins when you leave your home heading for the departure point of your trip. Otherwise, you could not file a claim if, say, you have an auto accident before you reach the cruise terminal. Always find out the exact expiration time and date of your policy. Some policies end two to three days before the departure date—the time when many last-minute reasons for canceling arise.

Ask your agent about exclusions for *preexisting conditions*—any illness or injury that existed before you purchased the policy that might lead you to cancel the trip. Try to secure the shortest possible exclusion period (in other words, the least number of days during which a recurring illness could flare up before your trip to force you to cancel). Many insurers will waive their preexisting condition exclusions if you purchase a policy within a short amount of time after placing a deposit on your trip (generally, seven to fourteen days).

You should also confirm that your policy covers supplier *failure* or *default*, not just *bankruptcy*. It is more common for travel companies simply to go out of business these days, than to file officially for bankruptcy.

Other common exclusions include cosmetic or elective surgery, venereal diseases, mental illnesses, dental problems, or even military orders to report as a reservist for active duty. One important exclusion in many policies is pregnancy. This means if you become pregnant after booking a cruise and purchasing trip cancellation insurance, your policy may not allow you to cancel the trip for full coverage. If you regularly engage in *high risk* activities such as skydiving, scuba diving, or competitive sports, find out whether your policy would cover you if an injury resulting from these activities leads to your trip cancellation.

While many policies do cover you in the event of a terrorist incident (usually if your destination was attacked within thirty days of your arrival date), they almost never insure losses caused by war or the mere threat of a war or terrorist incident. Terrorism clauses in travel insurance policies can include surprising loopholes. Some insurers will not pay claims if you travel to a destination targeted recently by terrorists (*i.e.*, *Access America* currently excludes Bali).

Trip Delay/Trip Interruption Insurance
This type of insurance protects you during the trip, reimbursing you for travel expenses resulting from delays, changes, or the

sudden end of your trip. It also covers you for injuries, accidents, or other events that cause you to change your itinerary once the trip is underway.

Basic trip interruption insurance plans reimburse you for the following added expenses:

- *change fees* for your airline ticket if you must return home for any covered reason;
- any unused prepaid deposits or trip expenses;
- additional living expenses if the trip is delayed; or,
- if you leave the trip for an allowed reason but wish to return before the tour or cruise ends, many policies will pay for a coach-class airline ticket for your return.

Many policies also cover emergency medical transportation or evacuation costs if you suffer a medical emergency during the trip. Read the fine print carefully, as many such clauses provide only for the expenses involved in moving you to the nearest *medically appropriate* facility. This means that you *could* be left at the hospital in the next foreign port on the cruise itinerary, rather than returned home to your local hospital in the United States.

Finally, many trip interruption policies pay for *repatriation of remains* or the additional costs of returning your body home if you die during the trip. While the prospect of dying on vacation is an unpleasant thought, this coverage will help your survivors pay for the paperwork and transportation costs of transferring your remains from another country back to the United States for burial or cremation—expenses that can easily total several thousand dollars.

In addition, many other nations have strict regulations regarding the release of human remains for transport outside their borders. In these cases, having repatriation of remains coverage will help to convince officials that your survivors have the financial means to claim and transfer your remains to the U.S.

Medical and Accident Insurance

This type of insurance makes the most sense for travelers who believe they (or the family members, partners, and companions traveling with them) have a significant chance of becoming ill or injured before or during the trip. It also works well if your planned trip will last longer than usual (for instance, an around-the-world cruise) or if you cannot easily handle losing the entire cost of your trip if something happens.

Many travel insurance policies include coverage if you become ill or injured during your trip. Usually, *accident insurance* and *sickness insurance* will be bundled together, although the coverage limits and exclusions may be different.

> ### Travel Tip
>
> Medical and accident insurance policies are best for travelers who have limited access to standard health coverage or whose existing health policies do not extend to travel outside the United States.

Travel Accident Insurance

This type of coverage typically reimburses to a maximum limit for the medical expenses that result if you are injured on the trip, including physician and hospital charges, ambulance transportation, x-rays, medical tests, and medications. Be prepared for major exclusions to appear in the fine print of this coverage, however. Many such policies have low limits ($10,000 per trip, for example). Your own health or auto insurance might actually provide more coverage for your injuries.

The sickness/hospitalization clauses in your travel insurance will apply if you become ill during the trip and you receive medical attention during or immediately following the trip. Many basic policies pay only a small amount of these medical expenses per day (with hospitalization required before you qualify for reimbursement). Some comprehensive coverage will apply to all types of medical expenses incurred while you are on the road. Most policies have a low overall limit on medical or hospitalization reimbursements (again, $5,000 per trip is one example). They may have strict preexisting condition exclusions, which may apply only for a set period of time (for instance, any costs for treatment sought within sixty to ninety days of falling ill).

Travel Tip

If you must file a travel insurance claim, check the fine print for reporting deadlines. For example, some policies will not pay unless you file a claim within seventy-two hours of your loss.

Accidental Death and Dismemberment Insurance (AD&D)

This insurance coverage provides a maximum amount of money that you can recover if you suffer major injuries while traveling. The insurance company will pay you a prorated amount of the maximum award based on the nature of your injuries.

Example:

Your policy has a maximum accidental death and dismemberment insurance (AD&D) level of $100,000 and you lose both eyes or both legs in an accident. It is likely you would be paid the full $100,000. However, if you lose only one hand, you might be paid only $25,000.

Many AD&D policies only apply to accidents that happen while you are traveling on a common carrier, such as an airline or bus, making flight insurance the most universal type of AD&D insurance in effect.

BAGGAGE INSURANCE

While lost, delayed, damaged, or stolen baggage complaints are some of the most common war stories told by weary travelers, the truth is that baggage protection insurance is rarely worth the expense, as many travelers' homeowners or renter's insurance already covers such losses. Additionally, if the luggage problem is the fault of an airline or other common carrier, then typically that supplier holds the chief responsibility for paying you for the loss, delay, damage, or theft of your baggage.

When you review the baggage protection clauses in different travel insurance policies, note that many of these clauses contain serious limitations. For example, most travel insurers put a strict cap on reimbursements to travelers whose lost, stolen, or damaged baggage contains computer equipment, cameras, watches, jewelry, and similar valuables. Serious weight is given to the wear and tear of the baggage and its contents, in an effort to keep claims payments low.

Baggage Delay Insurance

This insurance coverage reimburses you for any personal items or other necessities that you were forced to buy when your baggage did not arrive on time at your destination. This type of clause generally carries extremely low limits (sometimes a maximum of only $100) and your baggage must be delayed for more than twenty-four hours before the coverage begins.

Baggage protection insurance makes sense primarily for travelers who have no types of insurance that would protect their personal property if it is lost or stolen during a flight.

Travel Tip

If you regularly fly a particular airline, it pays to learn about the specific baggage exclusions in its policies.

TRAVEL ASSISTANCE SERVICES

Beyond these standard categories of coverage, some travel insurance policies will give you access to travel assistance services. These around-the-clock call centers are available for you to consult if you need information or referrals during the trip. They can be used for legal questions, translations, prescription drug services, credit card replacement reports, and other emergency needs.

TRAVEL INSURERS

ACCESS AMERICA
P.O. Box 71533
Richard, VA 23286
866-807-3982
www.accessamerica.com

Policy Details
- Covers supplier default if the policy is purchased within fourteen days of making the first payment towards the trip; travel suppliers that are excluded from coverage are listed at **www.accessamerica.com**.
- Covers *trip cancellation* for trip costs up to $30,000 if the policy is purchased within fourteen days of making the first trip payment; includes coverage for supplier default, illness or death of the traveler or a family member/companion, and labor disputes/natural disasters/weather conditions that cause a complete cessation of travel services for at least 24 consecutive hours, and employer termination (if employed for at least three years).
- Covers trip interruption for trip costs up to $30,000.
- Covers trip delay up to $200 per person (basic plan) or $500 per person (deluxe).
- Covers terrorism if the policy is purchased within fourteen days of making the first trip payment and if the traveler is scheduled to arrive within 30 days after the terrorist incident occurred.
- Includes a preexisting condition waiver (120 days) if the policy is purchased within fourteen days of making the first trip payment.
- Covers flight accidents up to $250,000 (basic) or $500,000 (deluxe).
- Covers baggage loss up to $500 per person (basic) or $1,000 (deluxe).
- Covers baggage delay up to $200 per person.

- Covers emergency medical expenses (including dental) up to $10,000 per person (basic) or $20,000 per person (deluxe).
- Covers emergency medical transportation up to $20,000 per person (basic) or $40,000 per person (deluxe).
- Includes rental car protection up to $25,000 per person (deluxe only).
- Includes after-hours emergency assistance.

Additional Information

Underwritten by *BCS Insurance Company* (rated A-); sold through 22,000 travel agencies; part of the Mondial Assistance Group, which is in turn part of the Allianz Insurance Group.

CSA TRAVEL PROTECTION
P.O. Box 939057
San Diego, CA 92193-9057
800-873-9855
www.csatravelprotection.com

Policy Details

- Does not cover supplier default (indefinite moratorium placed on this type of coverage after September 11).
- Covers trip cancellation for trip costs if the policy is purchased within seven days of making the first payment towards the trip (Gold Plan) or up to and including the date of final payment (Silver Plan); includes coverage for the illness/injury/death of the traveler or a family member as well as labor disputes/adverse weather/natural disasters that cause the cessation of all travel services.
- Covers trip interruption up to 150 % of the trip costs per policy.
- Covers trip delay up to $750 per person ($1,500 maximum).
- Covers terrorism in any foreign city at which the traveler is scheduled to arrive within thirty days of the terrorist incident.
- Includes a preexisting condition waiver (180 days) if the policy is purchased within seven days of making the first trip payment.
- Covers flight accidents up to $100,000 per person ($250,000 maximum).
- Covers baggage loss up to $1,000 per person ($2,000 maximum).
- Covers baggage delay up to $250 per person ($1,000 maximum).
- Covers emergency medical expenses up to $10,000 per person ($20,000 maximum); not available to Canadian residents.
- Covers emergency medical transportation with no limits.

- Includes rental car protection up to $25,000 per person; not available to residents of Oregon, New York, and Texas.

Additional Information

Underwritten by *OneBeacon Insurance Group* (rated "A"); general agency with administrator authority selling through 7,000 travel agencies.

TRAVEL GUARD INTERNATIONAL
1145 Clark Street
Stevens Point, WI 54481
800-826-4919
www.travelguard.com

Policy Details

- Covers supplier default if the policy is purchased within seven days of making the first payment towards the trip; travel suppliers that are excluded from coverage are listed at **www.travelguard.com**; company reserves the right to substitute cash reimbursement with a trip of equal value.
- Covers trip cancellation for trip costs if the policy is purchased within seven days of making the first trip payment; includes coverage for the illness/injury/death of the traveler or a family member, employer termination (if employed at least five years), and weather that cancels the trip.
- Covers trip interruption up to the trip costs ("ProtectAssist") or up to 150 % of the trip costs ("Cruise Tour & Travel").
- Covers trip delay up to $100 per day for five days maximum if the trip is delayed more than twelve hours (PA) or up to $200 per day for five days maximum if the trip is delayed more than six hours (CTT).
- Covers terrorism if the policy is purchased within seven days of making the first trip payment and if the traveler was scheduled to arrive in the destination within thirty days of the terrorist incident.
- Includes a preexisting condition waiver (sixty days) if the policy is purchased within seven days of making the first trip payment.
- Covers flight accidents up to $25,000, with option to increase coverage to $500,000.
- Covers baggage loss up to $1,000 per person, plus free "Bag Trak" service for one year.

- Covers baggage delay up to $100 per person (PA) or $200 per person (CAA) if the baggage is delayed more than 24 hours.
- Covers emergency medical expenses up to $10,000 per person.
- Covers emergency medical transportation up to $20,000 per person.
- Includes rental car protection up to $25,000.

Additional Information

Underwritten by *Insurance Company of North America*/ACE (rating not available); claims 60% of the U.S. travel insurance market with $100 million in annual sales via 16,000 travel agencies and 300 wholesalers (such as tour operators and cruise lines).

TRAVELEX
P.O. Box 641070
Omaha, NE 68164-7070
888-457-4602
www.travelex-insurance.com

Policy Details

- Covers supplier default up to $25,000 if the supplier ends service more than ten days after the effective date of the policy.
- Covers trip cancellation for trip costs up to $25,000; includes coverage for the illness/injury/death of the traveler or a family member/business partner/companion, as well as supplier default/ strikes/weather conditions that cause a cessation of travel for 48 consecutive hours or employer termination (if employed with a company for at least three years); not available to Oregon residents.
- Covers trip interruption under the same terms as trip cancellation.
- Covers trip delay up to $150 per day if the client is delayed more than three hours.
- Covers terrorism if the U.S. State Department issues a travel warning to the country the traveler is scheduled to visit.
- Includes a preexisting condition waiver if the policy is purchased within ten days of making the first trip payment.
- Covers flight accidents for the value of the flight.
- Covers baggage loss up to $1,000.
- Covers baggage delay up to $200.
- Covers emergency medical expenses up to $5,000.
- Covers emergency medical transportation up to $50,000.

Additional Information

Underwritten by *Old Republic Insurance Company* (rating not available); sold through 7,500 travel agencies.

TRAVEL INSURED INTERNATIONAL
52 S. Oakland Avenue
P.O. Box 280568
East Hartford, CT 06128
800-243-3174
www.travelinsured.com

Policy Details

- Covers supplier default up to $20,000 per person if the policy is purchased within seven days of making the first payment towards the trip.
- Covers trip cancellation for trip costs; includes coverage for the illness/injury/death of the traveler or a family member/companion/business partner, as well as labor strikes or weather conditions that cause the cessation of travel services for at least 48 consecutive hours and employer termination (if employed for at least three consecutive years).
- Covers trip interruption up to 150 % of the trip costs.
- Covers trip delay up to $300 if the trip is delayed more than six hours.
- Covers terrorism up to the trip costs if the U.S. State Department issues an official travel warning.
- Includes a preexisting condition waiver (six months) if the policy is purchased within seven days of making the first trip payment.
- Covers flight accidents up to $100,000 or $250,000, depending on the type of policy.
- Covers baggage loss up to $250 per article, with $500 maximum for the loss of jewelry, watches, and other types of valuables.
- Covers baggage delay up to $200 if delayed more than 24 hours.
- Covers emergency medical expenses up to $10,000.
- Covers emergency medical transportation up to $50,000.
- Includes after-hours emergency assistance.

chapter nine:
Travel Crimes and Scams

In South Carolina, a man received an unsolicited fax at his office promising vacation packages at prices he could not refuse. He called the phone number printed on the fax to book his getaway, which included first-class accommodations, complimentary breakfasts, and an invitation-only mini-cruise. When he arrived at the resort, however, he discovered that the cruise carried a mandatory $200 fee and, in order to check into his room and receive his breakfast coupons, he would be forced to attend a sales seminar on timeshares.

When a telemarketer contacted a woman in Florida with special travel deals, she told the caller that she was not quite ready to commit to a trip. The telemarketer persuaded her to mail in a deposit check for the trip, promising a full refund if she changed her mind. When she called later to cancel the reservation and recover her deposit, she was told that it was absolutely nonrefundable.

A Missouri couple purchased a five-star trip to the Bahamas with a discounted vacation certificate they had received in the mail. They arrived in the islands, however, to find a dilapidated room with no air conditioning, carpet, or easy beach access. "This whole vacation experience was a nightmare, and absolutely nothing like what was represented by the company," the wife told investigators with the *Federal Trade Commission* (FTC).

Every year, Americans lose billions of dollars in travel scams—from run-down hotels that are promoted as deluxe resorts to outright *pitch and run* frauds where the sales reps vanish overnight with client deposits. Also, growing concerns about crimes on the road—ranging from the occasional purse snatcher or pickpocket to fanatical terrorists targeting American travelers—have made consumers much more conscious of their surroundings and more cautious on their trips. This chapter gives you tips for preventing travel-related crimes and explain the avenues open to you for protecting your legal rights if you fall victim.

RECOGNIZING AND AVOIDING SCAMS

The primary rule for protecting yourself against travel scams is the age-old advice that, if an offer sounds too good to be true, it probably is. Many crooks snare consumers who become tempted by huge discounts that sound plausible, particularly since many travel suppliers today routinely offer booking bargains and last-minute deals to recover sales lost after the September 11 tragedies.

The following *red flags* indicate that you have been targeted as an easy mark by a travel scam artist.

- *The seller will not give you anything in writing describing the trip until you have paid first.* Always insist on receiving material in the mail before you pay any trip deposits or fees. Absolutely refuse to pay any money to a travel seller *before* you have this material in hand. Ask the seller to send you complete details about the trip, including:
  - the total price;
  - service charges and processing fees;
  - the components of the trip (particularly the specific hotels, airline flights, cruise ships, and other travel services involved);

♦ any penalties for canceling or changing the trip plans; and,

♦ blackout dates.

- *The seller pressures you to make an immediate decision.* Always refuse any high-pressure sales pitches that prevent you from shopping around with other travel retailers.

- *The seller demands your credit card number or bank account number over the phone.* Never give out your banking or credit card information over the phone unless you called the travel retailer yourself, you know the retailer, and you are completely confident in the company. With just your credit card number and expiration date, the most inexperienced scam artist can successfully make fraudulent charges on your credit card. With your bank account number, the scam artist can deduct or transfer funds from your account.

- *The seller tells you that you just won a prize or a trip in a contest that is news to you.* If you cannot remember registering for any sweepstakes, the chances are good that the promised trip or prize is a fraud or at least a gimmick with lots of hidden costs and conditions.

- *The seller says that you can claim your prize or trip by paying a small administrative fee.* The administrators

Travel Tip

To withdraw funds from a consumer's bank account over the phone, the seller must follow FTC regulations that require express authorization from the consumer that includes:

- written consent (such as a faxed authorization form or a canceled check) or a tape recording where the consumer states the date of the withdrawal;
- the amount of the withdrawal;
- the consumer's name;
- a telephone number the bank can call during business hours with questions; and,
- the date of the authorization.

of reputable contests and sweepstakes never require you to pay a fee to collect a prize (in fact, some state laws specifically prohibit this practice). Refuse to pay any amount of money to collect a promised prize or trip.

- *The seller asks you to make a bank transfer, send a certified check or money order, or prepare a check to be picked up by a courier.* By using cash equivalents or receiving funds using delivery methods other than the U.S. Postal Service, scam artists are trying to take advantage of perceived loopholes in federal regulations prohibiting fraud via phone and mail.

- *You cannot book the deal through any other travel retailer.* If you are told that you must purchase the trip directly from the seller—that the deal is so good that it cannot be booked through any other travel agent or retailer—chances are that something is wrong.

- *You must call a 900 number to book the trip.* It would be highly unusual for any reputable travel retailer to force customers to pay for the cost of their reservations calls, especially via 900 numbers that are notoriously expensive.

- *The seller refers to leading U.S. airlines or the world's best hotels instead of naming specific travel suppliers involved in the trip.* Scam artists use such references to mask the fact that very few (if any) reputable travel suppliers are involved in their trips. In particular, fraudulent vacation coupons will usually omit any supplier names, travel dates, and prices. Always ask for specific supplier names and contact those companies to determine if they honor the coupon or if they are involved in the trip you are being pitched.

- *The seller cannot give you references from suppliers or satisfied customers, or the references sound too good to be true.*

- *The seller does not belong to any professional travel trade association.* If the caller gives you the name of an association, contact the group's headquarters to determine if the company is a current member. Sometimes, scam artists join an organization briefly, begin printing the group's name and logo in their marketing materials, and then drop out.

- *The seller requires you to wait an extremely long time (several weeks or even months) before you can claim your prize or take your trip.*

Coupon Scam

Perhaps the most classic form of travel scam is the mailed certificate or coupon promising you a deeply discounted vacation. In grand language, the certificate describes the trip's benefits and very low price, without listing any specific travel dates or travel suppliers. To redeem the certificate, you will typically be directed to call a hotline number, where highly skilled telemarketers will attempt to collect money from you in order to redeem the certificate.

One version of the coupon scam is telling victims that they have been chosen to receive a trip at an amazingly low price—without telling them about the strings attached, such as hidden charges that add up to make the trip costing the same or more than the same trip purchased through a typical travel agent. Another wrinkle is the *trip to nowhere,* in which the coupon is actually worthless (the scam artist simply mails certificates and collects payments for thirty to sixty days before disappearing with the funds). A third variation is the phony prize drawing, in which you may be asked to pay the seller to claim a prize trip that is ultimately worth less than the amount you paid in the first place.

Because it is extremely difficult to track down and sue travel scam artists, your safest bet is avoiding any involvement with vacation certificates, coupons, and contests unless you specifically remember entering the sweepstakes.

Credit Cards and Debit Cards

Because more victims these days attempt to protect themselves by using their credit cards to pay for trips or prizes offered over the phone, scam artists now routinely make them wait at least sixty days before fulfilling the *order*. By doing so, they are attempting to prevent you from requesting a *charge back* on your credit card when the deal falls through. Under the terms of the *Fair Credit Billing Act*, you must dispute questionable charges within sixty days of the date you receive your credit card statement.

Even if your credit card company gives you a longer charge back period (some issuers give card holders up to a year to contest a charge), the scam artist may have fleeced enough consumers in sixty days to flee with the proceeds before you report the trouble to your credit card company.

For the same reasons, you should never use your debit card to purchase travel services, because the federal rules governing *charge back* periods for credit cards do not apply to debit cards. By giving the reservations agent (or scam artist) your debit card number and other banking information, you have, in effect, given away complete access to all accounts tied to that debit card.

Potential Timeshare Fraud

Since its beginnings in the U.S. in the 1970s, the *timeshare* industry has grown tremendously as an affordable way for consumers to stay at resort properties for rates that (over time) will save them money on their vacations. In the standard timeshare deal, the traveler pays a one-time sign-up fee, plus an annual maintenance fee, in exchange for the right to use a specific vacation property for a certain amount of time each year (typically, one week). Popular in vacation hot spots like Florida, California, and Hawaii, timeshares spread the cost of building and maintaining a resort property across a wider base of partial owners, making it possible for you to stay at a property that would otherwise be too expensive to rent or buy.

Many timeshare owners are lured into sales presentations after purchasing trips and timeshare stays at greatly reduced prices. Typically, you must sit through a presentation on buying timeshare property when you arrive for your stay. This is a presentation given by aggressive sales representatives who sometimes exceed their allotted time and may refuse to give the promised trip discount if you decide not to buy a time-share in the end.

In technical terms, any timeshare company that refuses to give you the bonus or discount rate offered before you attended the sales presentation may be guilty of fraud, breach of contract, or both. In practical terms, however, you will be hard-pressed to pursue the timeshare company for compensation. Your best options will be reporting the deceptive behavior to your state attorney general's office, the Better Business Bureau, and other local authorities, in hopes of putting the dishonest operation out of business.

If you decide to purchase a timeshare, remember that almost all timeshare agreements require a one-time sign-up fee plus the annual maintenance fee. Be sure to ask the timeshare company, as well as other owners in that timeshare property, how much the annual fees have increased over time (and may increase down the road). It is not uncommon for timeshare owners to report significant hikes in annual maintenance fees at some companies. The timeshare developer may charge its owners with additional special assessment fees if the company needs to rebuild its operating reserves for the resort. Get as much detail written into your timeshare contract regarding any fees you might be charged.

Cooling-Off Laws

If you purchase a timeshare but decide later that you made a mistake, many states now enforce *cooling-off laws* that allow you to rescind any timeshare purchase agreement. This can be done without penalty within a few days of signing it for a full refund of any fees you have already paid. (See the state-by-state *cooling-off laws* supplement at the end of this chapter to determine the protection in your particular state.)

Potential Charter Fraud

Charter operations form when a tour company enters into a long-term agreement with a charter air carrier in an attempt to attract customers with airfares that are much lower than the rates offered by major airlines. Typically, charter airlines provide transportation for travelers who have purchased a trip packaged by the affiliated tour operators. While many charter operators provide reliable low-cost travel packages, the field is filled with the collapse of several large charter companies (and others with shaky financial foundations).

The *Department of Transportation* (DOT) regulates charter operators with a complex set of rules requiring them either to post a bond or to deposit consumer funds in an escrow account. These DOT rules prevent overextended charter operators from taking payments from travelers and then canceling the charter flights or shutting their doors altogether. However, dishonest charter companies can circumvent these rules by fraudulently diverting funds from escrow accounts or simply not depositing consumer funds into the escrow accounts in the first place. When that happens, travelers have little or no recourse to recover their money.

If your charter flight is delayed or canceled, you must complain to the tour operator and ask that company for an adjustment or refund (rather than the charter airline itself). Although the charter operator bears responsibility in general for trip cancellations or delays, it

Know Before You Go

The DOT requires charter companies to file a prospectus explaining how their business is organized. Take the initial step of determining whether the charter operator you are dealing with has done this by calling the DOT's Consumer Affairs Office at 202-366-2220. Ask for the charter operator's prospectus number.

is usually not liable for any physical injuries or damage caused by the charter airline.

Travel Solicitations by Phone

When you receive travel solicitations by telephone, keep in mind that the telemarketer must tell you the following information at the beginning of the call:

- the seller's identity;
- the purpose of the call (selling your travel services);
- the nature of the goods or services being sold (a trip or travel discounts);
- the total price;
- any limitations or restrictions on the trip;
- the seller's policy on offering a refund, exchange, or cancellation;
- a full explanation of the refund policy, if the caller mentions refunds;
- that no purchase is necessary, if the offer is a prize;
- the odds of winning; and,
- toll-free number you can call to obtain contest entry information.

The telemarketer cannot call you before 8 a.m. or after 9 p.m. Finally, the seller should not call you again if you have told him previously that you wish to be put on his company's *no call list*.

Except for the prohibitions on mail and wire fraud that affect all types of scam artists, there is very little federal or state legislation designed to prevent fraudulent, *fly by night* travel retailers. As a result, travel scams always rank near the top of the FTC's annual lists of common consumer frauds.

DEALING WITH TRAVEL-RELATED CRIMES

"Crime takes no holiday," says veteran travel industry attorney Rodney Gould. In his work for a major national travel insurance company, he sees many different examples each year of the ways in which travelers fall prey to criminals during their trips. Here are three of his examples.

While touring Madrid on a seven-day packaged trip, a man lost his wallet to a pair of roving street criminals. While one man feigned tripping on the pavement and spilling ice cream on the tourist's clothes, his partner stepped over to help wipe off the ice cream and, at the same time, picked the tourist's pocket.

• • • • •

A woman asked workers at her hotel in St. Thomas to recommend a nearby inexpensive restaurant. She stopped by the restaurant during the day to inspect it, then returned that evening for dinner. On the way home, she was mugged.

• • • • •

Parents traveling on a ship with one of the world's most respected cruise lines placed their two-year-old child in the ship's day care center during the voyage. They decided upon returning home that the toddler was behaving strangely. They filed suit against the cruise line alleging sexual abuse.

Sometimes, the crimes faced by travelers obviously happen as a result of their own negligence and lack of caution. However, you can take the following steps to reduce the chances that you will fall victim to crimes on the road.

- Do not advertise your U.S. citizenship while abroad. Especially in today's aggravated climate, avoid outward displays (such as wearing red-white-and-blue clothing) that make it clear you are an American tourist.
- Avoid wearing jewelry on your trip.
- Do not carry more than the petty cash you will need at any given time.
- Keep your wallet in your front pocket (or do not carry it at all) or make a double loop if possible around your arm with your purse string.

- Keep a photocopy of your passport pages in a place separate from your actual passport, such as in your luggage or your pocket.
- As soon as you arrive in a new place, immediately find out the location of the nearest U.S. embassy or consulate.
- Read local English-language newspapers or watch the TV in your room in order to stay updated on local news.
- Listen to your inner voice. If you feel alarmed or threatened, do not feel embarrassed about leaving a place or returning to your hotel for safety.
- Know the fine print in your current homeowners', renter's, business, and health insurance policies for crimes on the road. Consider purchasing travel insurance for each trip.
- Report any crime immediately to local authorities, as well as your travel agent and any travel suppliers involved (such as the cruise line, tour company, or hotel). Keep a copy of any police reports or forms that describe what happened for your records.
- Always check (and obey) U.S. State Department travel advisories and warnings for hot spots around the world.

Beyond this advice, remember that many insurance policies (especially travel insurance) have exclusions and loopholes in the event of war, political unrest, or terrorism. Always check the details of your policies if you are concerned about your trip.

TRAVEL AGENT ID CARD MILLS

In the mid-1990's, several national companies began selling *travel agent kits* to consumers, promising in legally questionable language that consumers could use the travel agent identification cards contained in the kits to secure the travel discounts and perks traditionally reserved for professional travel agents.

Particularly since September 11, many travel suppliers that once extended these benefits have cracked down on the practice, even for full-time travel agents. Also, many suppliers now accept only a professional accreditation such as an identification card issued by the *International Airlines Travel Agent Network (IATAN)* based on the travel agent's proven record of selling travel.

Know Before You Go

Keep in mind that many card mill scams offer cards with an IATAN logo. However, many suppliers insist on approving only a card that has been issued *directly* by IATAN.

REPORT THE CRIME

Even if you believe that little can be done to help you recover your money lost in a travel scam or crime, or if you are embarrassed about reporting that you were *taken*, complain to local authorities as well as the following agencies.

The FTC estimates that one out of two U.S. consumers preyed upon by travel crooks fail to report the crime—a statistic that helps keep the crooks in business.

Federal Trade Commission
600 Pennsylvania Avenue, N.W.
Washington, DC 20580
ATTN: Consumer Protection
202-326-2222
www.ftc.gov

If you have fallen victim to a travel scam, contact the *National Fraud Information Center* (NFIC) immediately. The NFIC can help you file official legal complaints with federal agencies and give you advice on other steps that may be taken.

National Fraud Information Center
1701 K Street, N.W.
Suite 1200
Washington, DC 20006
800-876-7060
www.fraud.org

You can submit a complaint to your Congressman about any travel issue by visiting the website for the Consumer Travel Rights Center at **www.mytravelrights.com**. (The authors of this book founded this nonprofit organization in response to concerns expressed by federal agencies that traveling consumers do not always understand their rights or know the avenues available to them for filing a complaint.)

COOLING-OFF LAWS

California—within three days of signing
(Cal. Bus. & Prof. Code Sec.11024)

Connecticut—within three days of signing
(Conn. Gen. Stat. Sec. 42-103y)

Delaware—within five days of signing
(Del. Code Ann. tit. 6, Sec. 6-2824)

Florida—within ten days of signing
(Fla. Stat. Ann. Sec. 721.065)

Georgia—within seven days of signing
(Ga. Code Ann. Sec. 44-3-174)

Hawaii—within seven days of signing
(Haw. Rev. Stat. Sec. 514E-8)

Illinois—within five days of signing
(765 ILCS 101/10-10)

Indiana—within seventy-two hours of signing
(Ind. Code Sec. 32-32-3-7)

Louisiana—within ten days of signing
(La. Rev. Stat Ann. Sec. 9:1131.13)

Maine—within ten days of signing
(Me. Rev. Stat. Ann. tit., 33 Sec. 592)

Maryland—within ten days of signing
(Md. Code Sec. 11A-114)

Missouri—within five days of signing
(Mo. Rev. Stat. Sec. 407.620)

Montana—within three days of signing
(Mont. Code Ann. Sec. 37-53-304)

Nebraska—within three days of signing
(Neb. Rev. Stat. Sec. 76-1716)

Nevada—within five days of signing
(Nev. Rev. Stat. 119A.410)

New Mexico—within seven days of signing
(N.M. Stat. Ann. Sec. 47-11-5)

North Carolina—within five days of signing
(N.C. Gen. Stat. Sec. 93A-45)

Oregon—within five days of signing
(Or. Rev. Stat. Sec. 94.836)

Pennsylvania—within five days of signing
(Pa. Stat. Ann. Sec. 455.609)

Rhode Island—within three days of signing
(R.I. Gen. Laws Sec. 34-41-4.06)

South Carolina—within four days of signing
(S.C. Code Ann. Sec. 27-32-40)

Tennessee—within ten days, if you made an on-site inspection or within 15 days if you did not
(Tenn. Code Ann. Sec. 66-32-114)

Texas—within six days
(Tex. Prop. Code Ann. Sec. 221.041)

Utah—within five days
(Utah Code Ann. Sec. 57-19-12)

Vermont—within five days
(Vt. Stat. Ann. tit. 27, Sec. 607)

Virginia—within seven days
(Va. Code Ann. Sec. 55-376)

Washington—within seven days
    (Wash. Rev. Code Ann. Sec. 64.36.150)

West Virginia—within ten days .
    (W. Va. Code Sec. 36-9-5)

Wisconsin—within five days
    (Wis. Stat. Sec. 707.41)

(If your state has no *cooling off* period or if you realize after the period ends that you made a mistake, then your best bet may be suing the timeshare developer.)

chapter ten:
Discrimination in Travel

Discrimination happens every day in the travel industry. Sometimes, of course, the discrimination in question is a completely legal business practice. For example, an airline gate agent may give the last remaining upgrade to first-class seating to a business owner on the flight who is an elite member of the airline's frequent flier club, rather than the college student who is taking his first flight. In another instance, a tour operator may refuse to sell space on an extreme rafting cruise down the Colorado River to a seven-year-old child traveling with his parents based on safety concerns. Other types of discrimination, however, clearly violate U.S. federal or state laws. In those cases, assert your rights to their fullest to protect yourself from being treated unfairly.

Keep in mind that U.S. laws barring such unfair treatment do not apply outside of the United States. When traveling to foreign countries, you will have limited options to file a claim or take any legal action against the alleged discrimination. In addition, due to cultural differences, what you perceive as discrimination may actually be a time-honored tradition in your host country.

RACE, COLOR, NATIONAL ORIGIN, AND RELIGION LAWS

Because most travel suppliers based in or operating in the United States have facilities that qualify as *places of public accommodation* (such as hotels and restaurants) or fall under the definition of *common carriers* (airlines and cruise lines), they are governed by the *Civil Rights Act of 1964*. This Act prohibits these suppliers from discriminating against you in any way based on your race, color, national origin, or religion. (After September 11, a growing number of Arab-American citizens and Muslims reported harassment while traveling, including delays at security checkpoints and even their removal from airplanes based solely on their appearance.)

GENDER

While U.S. travel suppliers may not discriminate against travelers on the basis of gender, this prohibition does not apply in other countries where gender discrimination is an everyday fact. Women traveling alone may encounter problems reserving travel services (such as hotel rooms and rental cars) in some regions. They may be forced to follow local customs such as covering their heads, legs, and arms when walking in public.

Pregnant women may travel on most air carriers through the first eight months of pregnancy. During the ninth month, however, some airlines require a letter from an obstetrician/gynecologist dated one to three days before the flight that states the pregnant woman is physically fit to fly.

Although the *Civil Rights Act* does not protect against gender discrimination, some travelers have based their claims of gender bias in public accommodations on the 14th Amendment of the U.S. Constitution.

SEXUAL ORIENTATION

While a growing number of U.S. cities have adopted *fairness ordinances* prohibiting discrimination against gay, lesbian, bisexual, and transgendered (GLBT) persons, there is no federal law barring such discrimination. As a result, GLBT travelers will likely have little legal recourse unless the discrimination occurs in a city with a fairness ordinance in effect. In those cases, consult the city's legal department for a copy of the actual ordinance to determine how a complaint or lawsuit should be filed against the offending travel supplier.

Otherwise, the best legal option may be claiming that the travel supplier breached its contract with you or violated a legal duty to you. With cruises, for example, the company's refusing to provide a cabin to a same-sex couple that has a confirmed reservation and has followed all of the contract conditions (for instance, paying for the cabin and showing up at the pier on time for embarkation) would likely constitute a *breach of contract*.

Under a hotel's general duty to receive, hotels must provide accommodations to all travelers who are able to pay for the lodging. GLBT travelers can claim a breach of contract if they are refused accommodations even though they hold valid reservations and can pay for their hotel expenses.

Unless the GLBT traveler poses a direct physical threat to the safety of the other passengers aboard an airplane, cruise ship, train, motor coach, or other common carrier, the company must carry the traveler regardless of his or her sexual orientation.

AGE DISCRIMINATION

The *Civil Rights Act of 1964* does not address age discrimination. Actually, based on claims of potential safety hazards, some travel-related federal and state laws expressly allow certain types of age limits and restrictions For example, rental car companies *sometimes* do not rent to drivers over the age of 70 or under the age of 25. The laws that do exist allowing age discrimination generally are for younger travelers. However, unless the travel supplier's behavior specifically violates a state or local statute prohibiting age discrimination, you will have little recourse for a successful claim if you encounter such practices as a senior traveler.

Children and Airlines

Children under the age of five must be accompanied by a parent or guardian to travel on an airplane. The DOT permits passengers who have child safety seats that meet federal standards to use them on board without counting the seats against any limits for carry-on baggage (but only when the passenger has paid the additional airfare for the child). Only FAA-approved child safety seats with backs and sides qualify for use on board the airplane. Other child booster seats, harnesses, and safety vests may not be used. Passengers may hold a child less than two years old in their laps during the flight without being forced to pay an additional airfare for the child.

Children between the ages of 5 and 12 may fly without a parent or guardian, but the airlines typically impose additional restrictions on unaccompanied minors and usually charge extra fees. For example, some carriers require *unaccompanied minors* to take nonstop, direct flights and many airlines charge fees of $25–$75 or more. Children traveling with their parents or guardians sometimes receive discounts, but generally the airlines charge unaccompanied minors the full adult ticket fare for a given flight.

The parent or legal guardian must bring the minor to the airline ticket counter with a completed form showing the child's name, age, medical conditions, and other personal details, as well as the identity of the person approved to pick up the child at the end of the trip. The parent must sign a form confirming that the airline will not accept any responsibility of guardianship for the child during the trip. Then, the parent may escort the child through the security checkpoint to the departure gate or the airline may assign a staffer to walk the child to the gate. An airline attendant will also escort unaccompanied minors from one airport gate to another when making connections.

At the end of the final flight, unaccompanied minors leave the plane after other passengers because an attendant must escort them. A parent or legal guardian must be present at the arrival gate to pick up the minor, showing official identification that matches the information shown in the unaccompanied minor form filed at the departure airport. (If an approved person is not present at the arrival gate, then the airline may actually be forced to turn the child over to local social service authorities or the police.)

For more details regarding traveling with children, check the FAA's complete guidelines at **www.faa.gov/fsdo/phl/children.htm**.

Children and Hotels

Some hotels will not rent rooms to unaccompanied minors. Even if state and local laws do not specifically prohibit this practice, the hotel may view it as a violation of its duty. However, if the hotel does accept minors as guests,

Know Before You Go

The DOT's Office of Consumer Protection offers a free pamphlet— Kids and Teens in Flight. It contains a **Travel Card** that you can complete with flight information and contact details for the unaccompanied minor to carry. Contact them at:

Office of Consumer Protection
400 Seventh Street, S.W.
Dept. C-75
Washington, DC 20590
202-366-2220

then it must welcome minors, even if adults do not accompany them. A minor is legally responsible for the hotel expenses, even though he or she may be too young otherwise to form a legally recognized contract in that state. Some hotels have a strict *no children policy*, which is completely legal in many jurisdictions.

Children Traveling with a Parent or Guardian

Along with the recent changes in passport regulations, the federal government imposed much stricter rules for children traveling with only one parent. Due to growing concerns about child custody battles and child pornography cases, any parent or guardian traveling alone with his or her children (not accompanied by the other parent or guardian) should carry a notarized copy of each child's birth certificate, as well as a notarized note from the other parent or guardian stating that the traveling parent has permission to take each child on the trip.

In particular, immigration officials in Canada have taken great pains to enforce these rules, given their shared border with the United States. If you do not have these papers with you, expect to be delayed or held in custody until immigration officials can confirm your story.

PHYSICAL AND MENTAL DISABILITY LAWS

Two powerful U.S. laws prohibit discrimination against travelers who have physical or mental disabilities: the *Americans with Disabilities Act* (ADA) and the *Air Carrier Access Act of 1986* (ACAA). However, proving that your complaint crosses the line into illegal discrimination can be a difficult task, depending on how a court interprets the language of each law.

The ADA is the nation's most comprehensive civil rights law for persons with disabilities. Under the ADA's terms, you have a disability if you live with a physical or mental impairment that substantially limits one or more major life activities. The law gives disabled travelers the same rights and access to public facilities including travel agencies, hotels, motor coaches, and tour operator services as other Americans without disabilities. Travel suppliers cannot *deny* disabled travelers the right to participate in their services. They cannot offer them unequal or separate treatment.

Further, the ADA requires that *public accommodations* make reasonable changes to their facilities, policies, and practices in order to make themselves accessible to disabled travelers. These changes are judged reasonable if they can be readily made without fundamentally altering the nature of the goods or services provided. Examples include a ramp for travelers with wheelchairs or a policy that allows blind travelers to bring their guide dogs into a hotel restaurant.

The ACAA prohibits discrimination against disabled persons in air travel and requires air carriers to accommodate the needs of passengers with disabilities. The Department of Transportation (DOT) enforces regulations

Travel Tip

Several guidebooks for disabled travelers have been published. Seek additional information from the Society for Accessible Travel and Hospitality at **www.sath.org**.

under the ACAA that define the rights of disabled passengers and the responsibilities of airlines. In late 2004, the DOT began considering an expansion of the ACAA to cover non-U.S. airlines that operate in the United States.

Airlines

Airlines cannot refuse transportation to any traveler on the basis of physical or mental disability. However, an airline may refuse to allow a disabled traveler on a flight if carrying the traveler would pose a demonstrable safety hazard for the flight. In those cases, the airline must submit a detailed written explanation for its actions to the DOT.

An airline may not require disabled persons to provide advance notice that they will be traveling on a flight. However, airlines may ask for advance notice of as much as forty-eight hours for certain services that require preparation time (such as portable respirators). Also, airlines may not limit the number of disabled passengers on any given flight.

Except in very limited circumstances defined in the ACAA, airlines may not require a disabled passenger to travel with a companion or attendant. If the airline insists on a second person, but the disabled passenger does not agree, the airline can require an attendant, but cannot charge for transporting him or her.

Airlines may not bar anyone from any given seat based on a disability or require a disabled traveler to sit in a particular seat, except as mandated by *Federal Aviation Administration* (FAA) rules. The FAA will permit only those passengers who have the physical ability to perform emergency evacuation functions to sit in the exit rows.

When disabled travelers are boarding a flight, deplaning, or making connections, the airline must assist them in reasonable ways. While these travelers are inside the cabin, airline personnel must provide assistance but not *extensive personal services*. Disabled passengers' items stored in the cabin must meet FAA guidelines for stowing carry-on baggage, but assistive devices do not count toward the airline's limit on carry-on items. If the disabled traveler goes through the airline's pre-boarding process, then his or her wheelchair or other assistive devices take priority over carry-on items brought on board by other passengers and over checked luggage in the airplane's baggage compartment. Further, the airline must accept battery-powered wheelchairs (including the batteries) and any other luggage from a disabled traveler that might qualify otherwise as hazardous materials. The airline may not charge the disabled traveler any fees for doing so (though the carrier may charge for optional services, such as providing oxygen tanks).

Airplanes Delivered After 1992

Airplanes delivered after 1992 with at least thirty seats must have moveable aisle armrests on at least half of their aisle seats. Widebody airplanes (with at least two aisles) delivered after 1992 must also have accessible lavatories. Airplanes with at least 100 seats delivered after 1992 must set aside priority space to stow a passenger's folding wheelchair in the cabin.

Airplanes with more than sixty seats and an accessible lavatory must carry a wheelchair on board at all times (regardless of the delivery date). For flights on planes with more than sixty seats but no accessible lavatory, the airlines must add an onboard wheelchair if the disabled passenger gives at least forty-eight hours notice.

Airports

Airport authorities must ensure, under the ADA and ACAA, that airport terminals make the following services and facilities accessible to disabled travelers:

- parking near the terminal;
- restrooms;
- water fountains;
- medical aid facilities;
- travelers' aid stations;
- ticket counters or systems;
- baggage check-in and claim areas;
- jetways; and,
- mobile lounges.

Also, the terminals must have:

- text telephones and amplified telephones for use by travelers with speech or hearing impairments;
- level entry boarding ramps, lifts, or other methods of helping disabled travelers to board and deplane;
- data systems that can provide information to disabled travelers visually and orally; and,
- directional signs showing the location of airport facilities and services.

Privately-owned ground transportation and concessions selling goods and services to the public at airports must be accessible to disabled travelers. Also, major airports must have accessible shuttle vehicles to transport people between parking lots and terminals and moving walkways within and between terminals and gates.

Travel Tip

Request a copy of Access Travel: Airports. This publication is a free guide listing accessible services at more than 500 U.S. airports.

Consumer Information Center
Pueblo, CO 81009
800-FED-INFO
www.pueblo.gsa.gov

Travel Agencies and Tour Operators

Travel agencies and tour operators in the United States must abide by ADA guidelines to ensure that their places of business can accommodate disabled consumers. Even home-based travel agents must make the portion of their homes used for the business accessible.

If the agency's office is open to the public, then it must make reasonable accommodations for blind clients (such as having an employee available to guide the client inside the agency and to read any travel information aloud to them) and for clients in wheelchairs (for instance, entry doors that are at least 32 inches wide). Further, at least one entrance (preferably the main door) must be completely accessible, so that disabled travelers can enter without difficulty. If that is not possible, the agency must post a sign indicating where the accessible entrance is located.

If the agency owns and operates its own parking spaces for clients, then accessible parking spaces must be provided for clients who display official *handicap tags* in their vehicles.

Travel retailers must allow disabled clients to bring their service animals (such as guide dogs) with them inside the retail location. The agency or operator may not deny service to any disabled person because the behavior that results from his specific disability may be unsettling to the retailer's employees or other clients.

Finally, retailers are not required to have their own text telephones or amplified telephones for hearing-impaired clients. Instead, they may use the *relay services* offered by telephone companies.

Motor coach operators must give disabled passengers the same rights and access as other travelers, including providing wheelchair lifts and tie downs. While motor coach companies are not required to *retrofit* all of their existing vehicles, they must have a sufficient supply of accessible motor coaches so that a disabled traveler is not unduly limited in choosing a tour. (The disabled traveler may prefer to follow the standard motor coach inside a wheelchair-accessible minivan, but federal rules do not permit this type of substitution.)

Hotels

Hotels in the U.S. must make their accommodations readily accessible for disabled guests. Hotels built since 1990 must conform to strict ADA guidelines, but older hotels (even historic inns and bed-and-breakfast homes) must renovate their facilities in every way that does not fundamentally alter the character of the property.

Hotels do not have to make every single room accessible, as long as the rooms that are retrofitted for disabled guests are clearly designated and are not inferior to the other rooms in the hotel. Examples of accessible hotel features include handrails on stairs, entry and exit ramps, emergency alarms with flashing lights, elevator panels with Braille or raised-lettering words and numbers, and wider doors and doorways in rooms to allow passage via wheelchair.

Also, hotels must make a percentage of their rooms (in each class of service) fully accessible, including lower bathroom counters and grab bars in the bathtub and near the toilet. For newly built hotels, 4% of the first 100 rooms (and 2% of the rooms above the first 100) must be wheelchair-accessible and include flashing lights or other visual alarms for people with hearing impairments.

Cruise Lines

Cruise ships that call on U.S. ports (even vessels that operate under the flags of other countries) must comply with ADA regulations in all places on board that are accessible to the public. These regulations require, for example, that all physical barriers (such as a change in grade greater than half an inch) must be removed if readily possible.

The biggest impairment to disabled passengers on a cruise ship can be the *sills* (raised entry barriers) on ship doorways.

While the sills are designed to prevent water from spilling into interior rooms when the outer deck gets wet, they can make getting around with a wheelchair almost impossible. Cruise lines must make ramps available, but they are not required to equip every doorway with a ramp.

While many of the newest cruise ships are very friendly to the needs of disabled travelers, some older vessels still in service can pose a challenge. Check with your travel agent or the cruise line to ask about a ship's *ADA* modification. Request the specific accommodations (*i.e.*, a cabin that is designed for and dedicated to passengers with wheelchairs, not a retrofitted cabin) that you will need to enjoy your trip.

Cruise lines may not require a disabled passenger to travel with a companion or attendant, but they do not have to provide any services *of a personal nature* if the disabled passenger travels alone.

Know Before You Go

Cruise Lines International offers *Cruise Guide for the Wheelchair Traveler*, a free brochure that you can request at:

Cruise Line International
500 Fifth Avenue, Suite 1407
New York, NY 10110
212-921-0066
www.cruising.org/planyourcruise/guides/
wheelchair.cfm

SMOKING

Since 1990, FAA regulations have expressly prohibited smoking on domestic flights shorter than six hours (including Alaska, Hawaii, Alaska, Puerto Rico, and the U.S. Virgin Islands). These rules apply to any airline flying these routes, regardless of whether the airline has its headquarters in the United States. Today, the great majority of international flights are also smoke-free.

While more cities and states have banned smoking in public areas (such as California's ban on smoking in bars and hotel lobbies), travel suppliers are generally acting voluntarily when they prohibit smoking in their facilities, as few laws require smoke-free facilities.

PETS

Except for service animals such as guide dogs for blind travelers, travel suppliers such as hotels and rental car companies have no legal obligation to accept or provide for pets traveling with their owners. If you plan to travel with your pet, ask your travel agent or the suppliers about their pet acceptance policies, and get the policies in writing before you leave. (The supplier may be guilty of *breach of contract* if it changes its response once you arrive with your pet in hand.)

On most airlines, dogs and cats and certain other domesticated animals may travel with you as excess baggage stored in a pet carrier inside the airplane's cargo hold. In some cases, pets small enough to be comfortable in a pet carrier that fits under an airline seat may be treated as carry-on baggage. However, some airlines allow only one carried-on pet for the entire airplane, so you should make your reservations well in advance of your trip (and get the confirmation in writing). The airline may charge you a fee for transporting the pet, even if it is treated as carry-on baggage. (Also, expect concerns from other passengers regarding allergies, noise, and sanitation.)

Pets traveling as checked baggage (on the same flights as their owners) or as cargo (without their owners) fall under the *Animal Welfare Act*. The pet must be at least eight weeks old, fully weaned, and kept in an approved carrier or kennel that meets size, sanitation, ventilation, and capacity standards. The airline must provide water at least once every twelve hours and food every twenty-four hours. You must provide the airline with written instructions on feeding, watering, and administering medications (along with written assurances that you fed and gave water to your pet within four hours of the flight's scheduled departure).

Many airlines have their own pet policies beyond the requirements of the *Animal Welfare Act*. For instance, you may be asked to provide an updated certificate of health for your pet. Also, airlines are not required to guarantee that your pet will travel on the same flights that you do, as some smaller airplanes have limited pressurized cargo space and cannot accommodate animals.

In 2003, the major airlines continued wrangling with the federal government fighting proposed changes in the rules governing pets on airplanes. You should definitely check with your travel agent or the airline for the latest regulations.

If you are taking your pet with you to another country, many nations have quarantine laws for animals entering from the United States that may require stays of as long as six months. Hawaii also enforces strict animal quarantine rules in an effort to keep rabies out of its territory. Always check with your travel agent or the U.S. embassy or consulate of the country you are visiting to determine the quarantine requirements. Because transported animals are legally considered cargo or checked baggage, the airline's liability limits in the event of your pet's injury or death are the same as for your suitcases (generally, $2,500 or less). Despite your mental anguish and emotional distress, most courts will deny claims that exceed the basic cargo and baggage limits.

Hotels have no legal obligation to accept pets, as long as this rule is enforced fairly and completely. AAA offers pet books listing pet-friendly hotels around the U.S. and Canada.

• • • • •

If you believe you may have been discriminated against while traveling, you should consider filing a complaint with the U.S. Justice Department or Transportation Department. Also, you may bring a private lawsuit on the basis of the *Civil Rights Act* against the offending supplier. A growing number of cities now have ordinances prohibiting discrimination on these grounds as well.

Glossary

This glossary contains basic travel terms that are considered essential for understanding commonly used travel documents and brochures. Even simple words like *double* and *net* have special meanings when used in a travel context.

A

add-on. A tour feature not included in the basic price.

add-on fare. An additional amount added to a gateway fare for travelers departing from other cities. (For example, a tour operator selling trips to Ireland with a gateway fare from New York City may have an *add-on fare* for clients to connect into New York from Atlanta or Boston.)

aft. Towards the rear of a ship.

air/sea fare. Airfare offered as part of a cruise reservation.

airport access fee. A fee paid by car rental companies located off the airport premises for the privilege of operating their shuttle vans on airport grounds. Typically, these fees are passed on to consumers.

airport code. See *city code.*

airport recoupment fee. A fee paid by car rental companies located on airport premises for the privilege of conducting business and operating their shuttle vans on airport groups. Typically, these fees are passed on to consumers.

all-inclusive. A price that includes most major types of travel expenses (lodging, meals, entertainment) in a single rate.

American Plan. A meal plan that includes breakfast, lunch, and dinner.

astern. At or toward the stern of a ship.

B

back-to-back ticketing. A prohibited airline ticketing strategy in which a passenger purchases two discounted round-trip tickets between the same cities but in opposite directions, with the goal of using parts of each round-trip ticket to pay less than the cost of a single round-trip ticket at the regular fare.

baggage allowance. The weight or volume of baggage that may be carried or checked by a passenger without paying additional charges.

bailee. A person who receives personal property from another as a bailment.

bailment. The delivery of personal property by one person to another who holds the property for a certain purpose under a contract (generally applies when a hotel holds personal property left in the room by a guest who has not yet paid his bill).

bailor. A person who delivers personal property from another as a bailment.

bait and switch pricing. A sales practice whereby a seller advertises a lower-priced product to lure customers only to solicit them to buy a higher-priced product.

bankruptcy. The legal condition in which a person or business is relieved of most debts and undergoes a judicially supervised reorganization or liquidation for the benefit of creditors.

base fare. The fare without taxes and other supplemental charges.

bereavement fare. A discounted price offered by an airline to a passenger who is traveling because a close relative has died.

berth. Bed on a cruise ship, usually attached to the wall.

blacklisted. The practice of being included on a list of persons or businesses that that are disapproved for doing business.

blackout date. A specific date when travel on certain discounted fares is not permitted (usually holidays).

blocked space. A reserved number of rooms, seats, or other space held in advance for the purpose of selling those rooms or seats as part of a convention or tour package.

boarding pass. An official form or card given to a passenger showing the seat assignment, boarding time, and other details.

bookable site. A website that allows customers to search for travel services and products, confirm reservations, and submit payments directly via the site.

bow. The front or forward of a ship.

breach of contract. Violation of a contractual obligation by failing to perform one's own promise or by interfering with another party's performance.

bucket shop. See *consolidator.*

bulk fare. A net fare for a certain number of seats.

bumping. Being denied boarding on an airplane because other passengers have been given higher priority to travel on an over-booked flight.

business class. A class of airline service between first class and economy or coach class, usually including larger seats and free alcoholic drinks.

C

cabin. A sleeping room on a ship, or the interior of an airplane.

cancellation penalty waiver. Permission given to a passenger by the cruise line or other travel supplier to cancel a trip without paying any penalties.

capacity controlled. A situation in which space or seating is limited.

CAPPS II (Computer-Assisted Passenger Pre-Screening System). A planned national security screening service by which travelers are judged as risks based on their demographic profiles and financial records.

carrier. Any travel supplier that transports passengers and/or freight, such as an airline, railroad, or motor coach company.

change of equipment. The switching of aircraft for a scheduled flight without changing the flight numbers.

change of gauge. See *change of equipment.*

chargeback. A request by a credit card holder to reverse or refuse a charge because the purchased product or service was not delivered as promised.

charter. A trip aboard an airplane, cruise ship, motor coach, or other mode of transportation solely for members of a specific group.

city code. The three-letter designation given to a specific city by airlines and government authorities.

city pair. An originating city and a destination city on any given itinerary.

city ticket office. A sales office for an airline that is located outside the airport.

closed date. A date on which no service is available because the travel supplier is completely booked.

coach class. The section of an airplane with standard service for passengers.

code of the seas. The general principles of maritime law that govern the operations of ships and their crews.

code sharing. The operation of a flight by one airline in the name of another airline working together in a partnership to share expenses and marketing tasks.

common carrier. A person or company in the business of transporting people or goods for a fee.

common law duty. An obligation that results from judicial decisions rather than statutes or constitutions.

comparative negligence. One's own negligence that proportionally reduces any damages that might be recovered from any person or business being sued.

compensatory damages. Money that is sufficient in amount to compensate an injured person for a suffered loss.

computerized reservation system. The electronic reservations network used by travel agents and travel websites to sell travel.

concourse. A passageway or corridor in an airport.

confirmed reservation. A reservation that has been acknowledged and accepted by a travel supplier (but not necessarily paid).

connecting flight. The changing of planes on a single flight itinerary.

consolidator. A person or company that purchases a certain inventory of seats or space at special rates to resell to travel agents and consumers, usually at prices that remain below regular rates.

contract. An agreement between two or more parties creating obligations that are enforceable or otherwise recognizable at law.

contract of carriage. The legal agreement between a common carrier and its customers.

continental breakfast. A simple breakfast with rolls and coffee, and sometimes juice and fruit.

corporate rate. A price offered to business clients in general or to a specific company that has negotiated the rate with the supplier.

coupon broker. A person or company that purchases and re-sells frequent flier awards (usually in violation of airline rules).

cross-border ticketing. The process of issuing a ticket that makes it appear that the trip begins outside the country where the real itinerary starts. Generally, prohibited practice that attempts to take advantage of lower fares or a better currency exchange rate outside the traveler's country.

cut-off date. The last date by which reservations must be made.

D

day rate. A discounted rate offered by hotels to customers who will occupy the room only during daytime hours.

debark. To disembark or get off an airplane or cruise ship.

deck plan. The ship diagram displaying cabins, public areas, and other sections of the vessel.

denied boarding compensation. The payment offered to air-line passengers who have been *bumped* involuntarily from a flight.

departure tax. A government fee levied on departing travelers, usually when they leave the country for the last time.

deplane. To get off a plane.

direct booking. A travel reservation made directly with a supplier by the customer without the assistance of a travel agent or other intermediary.

direct flight. A flight that does not require passengers to change airplanes (though it may, indeed, make stops).

disembark. To get off a cruise ship.

display bias. The practice by which the owner of a computerized reservation system or travel website designs the system or site so that certain travel suppliers' products and services are shown first or more often.

distressed inventory. Products or services that are in danger of expiring or otherwise losing their value to the point that their prices must be reduced for quicker sales.

double. A room shared by two people that contains one double bed.

double booking. The practice of confirming two or more reservations when only one will be used.

double-double. A room with two double beds.

double occupancy. The rate charged when two people occupy a room or cabin (usually quoted per person).

driver-guide. A person hired to drive a vehicle for travelers and point out places of interest in a destination.

drop-off charges. The fees charged when a renter of a vehicle does not return it to the original rental location.

duty-free. Not subject to tax.

duty of care. A legal relationship arising from a standard of care that, if violated, subjects the offending party to liability.

duty to receive. A legal relationship arising from the obligation to accept custody of persons or goods that, if violated, subjects the offending party to liability.

E

e-ticket. An *electronic ticket* or a ticket for transportation or other travel services that is stored in computer systems rather than printed tickets or records.

early departure fee. A charge imposed on a traveler for leaving a hotel earlier than the departure date given when the reservation was made.

economy class. See *coach class.*

embark. To go or get on board.

energy surcharge. A fee imposed on a guest by a hotel to cover rising utility costs at the hotel.

enplane. To go aboard an airplane.

en route. While traveling.

escorted tour. A tour that includes the services of a tour escort or guide.

escrow account. A bank account, generally held in the name of the depositor and an escrow agent, that is returnable to the depositor or paid to a third person on the fulfillment of specific conditions.

European plan. A meal plan in which no meals are included in the hotel rate.

excursion fare. A round-trip airfare with restrictions such as minimum and maximum stays and advance purchase requirements.

extended stay. A hotel stay of seven or more nights.

F

Fair Credit Billing Act. A federal law that eases the correction of billing errors by credit card companies and makes those companies more responsible for the quality of goods purchased by cardholders. (15 USCA Sections 1666-1666j.)

fairness ordinances. State or local statutes that prohibit discriminatory practices.

family plan. A travel policy offering family members discounted or free rates.

fare. Price.

fare basis. The code (a letter, letters, or letters and numbers) assigned to a specific fare and printed on the airline ticket.

fiduciary duty. An obligation of utmost good faith and trust owed by one who must exercise a high standard of care in managing another person's property or money to the beneficiary (one designated to receive money, services, or advice from the fiduciary).

first class. The best and most expensive seats and services.

first sitting. The earlier of two standard meal times aboard a cruise ship.

FIT tour. A pre-packaged vacation sold to individual travelers (the acronym is an outdated reference to Frequent Independent Travel or Foreign Independent Travel).

flag carrier. The national airline of a country.

flat rate. The basic price without any discounts.

fly-drive. A packaged vacation that includes airfare, car rentals, and (usually) lodging at a combined price.

force majeure. A contract term describing an event that cannot be predicted or controlled by the supplier, such as natural disasters or war.

foreign exchange conversion fee. A charge imposed on a consumer who exchanges currency or who makes a purchase in another country using his credit card.

forum selection clause. A contractual provision in which the parties establish the place (such as the country, state, or type of court) for specified litigation between them.

full board. See *American Plan*.

fuel plan option. A program offered by car rental companies in which renters may purchase fuel at a favorable price to refill their vehicles upon return, avoiding the need for them to purchase gas on their own.

full-fare ticket. An airline ticket purchased at its full price with no discounts or reductions in price.

full pension. See *American Plan*.

G

gangway. The ramp on which travelers enter and leave a ship.

gateway city. The city from which international flights or trips depart.

gateway fare. The basic fare offered on a trip from a gateway city.

Goods and Services Tax (GST). A national tax imposed in Canada on most goods and services purchased in that country.

green card. A federal registration card certifying a resident alien's status as a permanent U.S. resident.

group leader. The person who organizes and promotes a tour but acts as a volunteer rather than a paid agent or employee of the tour operator, such as the elected president of a senior citizens organization.

guaranteed reservation. A reservation that is both confirmed and paid for.

guaranteed share. A rate confirmed for a single traveler in the event that the supplier (or the traveler) does not find a roommate before the trip begins.

H

half board. A meal plan that includes breakfast and either lunch or dinner.

half pension. See *half board*.

hidden-city ticketing. A prohibited airline ticketing strategy in which a passenger purchases a ticket to a destination at a lower fare but deplanes at a connecting city that is the passenger's true destination.

high season. The period of the year during which prices and demand are the highest for a given destination.

hold. A temporary reduction in available credit when a cardholder makes a purchase with a credit card.

hotel voucher. A coupon that confirms payment has been made for a traveler for lodging at a hotel.

hub. An airport used as a major connecting point.

hub and spoke. A system for coordinating airline flights with selected cities serving as central points to which many flights from other cities are scheduled.

I

implied warranty of suitability. An express or implied promise that the property or service in a contract is suitable for the particular purpose desired by the buyer.

in transit. While traveling.

incidentals. Minor expenses that have not been included in the base rate for a hotel stay or other travel services.

inclusive. The single package rate charged by a hotel, resort, cruise ship, or other supplier for accommodations, meals, and other basic amenities.

independent tour. A tour that does not include the services of a tour escort or guide.

inside cabin. A cabin on a cruise ship that does not have a porthole or window.

interline. The ability to transfer passengers or baggage among different airlines.

intermodal. Involving two or more forms of transportation, such as air and sea.

International Driver's Permit (IDP). A globally recognized driving permit issued generally to travelers who hold a valid drivers' license in their home country.

K

king room. A room with a king-size bed.

L

land-only rate. A price that includes land-based services such as ground transportation and lodging but not air or sea transportation.

late charges. Charges incurred by the guest too late to be included in the hotel bill upon check-out.

late check-out fee. A charge imposed by a hotel when a guest leaves his room after the posted check-out deadline.

layover. The period of time during which a traveler changes airplanes, trains, or other forms of transportation.

leeward. The direction away from the wind.

leg. Segment, portion, or part.

letter of no record. A document issued by state authorities showing a person's name, date of birth, and a statement showing the years that were searched for your birth record, and the fact that there is no birth certificate on file.

lido deck. The deck on a cruise ship surrounding a swimming pool.

load factor. The percentage of capacity sold out of available seats or cabins for a particular carrier.

local guide. A person hired to conduct tours and point out places of interest in a destination.

local host. A person hired to represent the tour operator to supervise local arrangements for travelers, but who does not conduct tours personally.

loss damage waiver (LDW). An agreement by a car rental company that it will take responsibility for collision damages or vehicle loss in exchange for an additional daily fee paid by the renter.

low season. The period of the year during which prices and demand are the lowest for a given destination.

M

manifest. List of passengers for an airline flight or cruise sailing.

maritime law. The body of law governing marine commerce and navigation, the transportation of persons and goods at sea, and marine affairs in general.

meeting fare. The discounted airfare given to travelers attending the same event.

minimum connecting time. The least amount of time required to change planes.

modified American plan. A meal plan that includes breakfast and dinner.

N

natural person. A human being, as distinguished from an artificial person created by law, such as a corporation.

net amount. The price paid to a supplier after commissions have been deducted.

net fare. See *net rate*.

net net. The net rate for a group.

net rate. The wholesale rate that is usually marked up for resale to consumers.

no-call list. A national or state directory of persons who have requested exemption from receiving calls from telemarketers.

no show. A traveler who does not arrive on time to check in for travel services and fails to cancel the reservation, resulting generally in charges for the traveler.

nonowners liability policy. A liability insurance policy purchased by a traveler who does not own a vehicle but who frequently rents cars to avoid the expense of purchasing daily coverage from the car rental company.

nonrefundable. Not eligible for any refund.

nonscheduled. A carrier that offers service at irregular times or at less frequent intervals than scheduled carriers.

nonstop. Transportation made without any stops or interruptions.

nontransferable. Not eligible to be used by or assigned to any other person than the traveler named on the ticket.

O

occupancy rate. The percentage of rooms or cabins occupied as compared to the total number of rooms available.

ocean front. A room directly facing the ocean.

ocean view. A room from which it is possible to see the ocean, located on the side of the hotel.

off-peak. The period of the year during which travel demand is slow for a given destination.

one-way. A trip from an origin to a destination without a return.

open ticket. A ticket without reserved dates because the traveler is not sure about the dates of travel.

open seating. Access to any seat or table because they have not been preassigned to specific persons.

option date. The date by which payment for travel services must be made or the reservations will be canceled.

originating city. The city from which a trip begins.

outside sales agent. A commissioned salesperson who solicits business for a travel agent or other retailer.

outside cabin. A cabin on a cruise ship that includes a porthole, window, or veranda.

overbooking. The deliberate or mistaken confirmation of more reservations than available seats, rooms, or cabins.

P

passenger name record (PNR). The traveler's data contained within a reservations record, including name, address, phone number, and other details.

passport. An internationally recognized travel document certifying the identity and nationality of the bearer.

pat down search. A more thorough examination of a traveler by a security screener or guard, in which the officer pats areas of the traveler's body in an effort to discover weapons or contraband.

pax. Passengers.

PC reference number. An identification number issued by the Public Charter Office of the U.S. Transportation Department certifying that a travel package meets the federal requirements for selling a charter trip.

peak fare. The price charged during high season.

peak season. High season.

per diem. The per-day maximum amount for reimbursing travel expenses for corporate or government travelers, or the per-day charge for travelers buying a cruise, tour, or vacation package.

per-mile fee. A charge imposed by a car rental company for each mile that the renter drives a vehicle beyond the maximum number of miles allowed in the rental agreement.

personal accident and effects insurance (PAE). A policy offered by car rental companies that combines the coverage of personal accident insurance (PAI) and personal effects coverage (PEC).

personal accident insurance (PAI). A policy offered by car rental companies that pays medical and ambulance bills for drivers and passengers in a rental car that result from an accident.

personal effects coverage (PEC). A policy offered by car rental companies that covers the driver's personal belongings if they are lost or damaged due to theft or accident involving the rental car.

pick-up. The number of hotel rooms actually used out of a reserved block of rooms.

pitch. The distance between seats on an airplane or other vessel.

pitch and run. A travel scam in which a promoter solicits trip deposits from consumers and then vanishes with the money without delivering any travel services.

point of origin. The location at which a trip begins.

point to point. A type of ticketing in which individual airfares are purchased from city to city to reach a final destination.

point-beyond ticketing. *See hidden-city ticketing.*

port. The left side of an airplane or cruise ship; also, the docking facility for cruise ships.

port charges. Government fees levied on cruise passengers.

port of call. A scheduled place where a ship stops on its itinerary.

port of entry. The designated port where passengers first enter a country.

porterage. The service of baggage handling.

positioning. The moving of an airplane, cruise ship, or other vessel to a new location from which it will begin a new series of trips (also called *repositioning*).

positive space. A confirmed reservation.

pp. Per person.

preexisting condition. A condition that existed before an insurance policy was issued, such as a chronic illness.

pre/post tours. Additional days or vacation packages that can be added to the beginning or end of a convention, cruise, or tour for an extra charge.

prepaid. Paid in advance.

prepaid ticket. A form used when a person in one city wants to buy an airline ticket (usually for another traveler) that will be issued at the airport in another city (or within the same city if the departure is within 24 hours).

principal. One who authorizes another to act on his or her behalf as an agent.

promotional fare. Significantly discounted price offered by a supplier to draw additional traffic.

proof of identity. A legal document attesting to the identity of the bearer.

proof of nationality. A legal document attesting to the nationality of the bearer.

Provincial Sales Tax (PST). A tax imposed by certain provinces in Canada on most goods and services purchased within their borders.

prow. Toward the front part of a ship.

published fare. A price specifically published in the carrier's official database for a given flight.

Q

quad. A room for four people.

queen room. A room with a queen-size bed.

R

rack rate. The regular published rate that may be upgraded on arrival at no additional charge.

record locator number. *See passenger name record.*

red-eye flight. A flight scheduled late at night or during early morning hours, usually at a significant discount.

regular fare. The price without any restrictions.

reissue. To write a new ticket based on changes in travel plans.

room block. Rooms reserved for a group.

room night. One room used for one night.

room rate. The amount charged by a hotel for a single night's stay in a given room.

round-trip. A trip to a destination with a return back to the originating city; in airfares, the term also means that the same fare applies in both directions.

run of the house rate. *See rack rate.*

S

scheduled carrier. A carrier that publishes its timetable for providing services.

seat rotation. The system used on tours via which passengers change seats regularly for an equal opportunity for viewing from the best seats.

second sitting. The later of two standard meals times aboard a cruise ship.

secondary insurance coverage. An insurance policy that will apply only when other primary sources of coverage have been exhausted.

security agreement. A surety bond or escrow account offered by a travel supplier as a guarantee or protection for travelers' deposits and payments.

seller of travel laws. State statutes governing the registration, operations, and financial practices of travel agents and suppliers.

service charge. A fee added to a bill to cover the cost of tipping or other charges; also, the fee charged by many travel agents to make reservations, prepare tickets, and conduct other business for clients.

share fare. The price given to single travelers who are willing to share accommodations.

shore excursion. Sightseeing tours offered at ports of call during a cruise for an additional charge.

shoulder season. The weeks leading up to and falling immediately after the high season in a given destination.

single. A room or cabin for one person.

single supplement. The additional fee added to the double occupancy rate if a passenger is traveling alone.

soft departure. A cruise sailing or tour departure with a low number of bookings.

soft opening. The time before the grand opening of a hotel or resort when guests may stay with limited service available.

special assessment fee. Additional charges imposed by a time-share developer upon the owners in a development if the developer must increase its reserves.

special service requirement. A request for specific airline action, such as wheelchair transfers or a kosher inflight meal.

standard room. A basic room in a hotel.

standby. Attempting to travel via a wait list seeking an available seat or with a ticket with a reduced fare that does not allow the traveler to make advance reservations.

starboard. The right side of an airplane or cruise ship.

stem. The bow of the ship.

stern. The aft or rear of the ship.

stopover. A deliberate interruption of an itinerary.

supplementary liability insurance. Additional liability coverage purchased by a traveler in addition to any existing liability policies.

T

tamper evident tag. A special tag placed on luggage that will show signs of damage if a suitcase is opened after the tag is put in place.

terms and conditions. The paragraphs in a contract (or on a website) describing the responsibilities and liabilities of the supplier and of travelers.

theft insurance. A policy offered by car rental companies that covers your personal belongings if they are lost or damaged due to theft or accident involving the rental car.

through fare. A price for traveling from the originating city all the way to the final destination.

through passenger. A traveler who is not departing at a given time because he or she is waiting to travel onward to a final destination.

throwaway ticketing. *See hidden-city ticketing.*

ticket. The written or printed contract governing promised travel services.

ticket designator. The code shown on a ticket indicating a discount.

total quoted rental price. The estimated charge for renting a car that includes the basic daily rate as well as any additional insurance or rental fees.

tour conductor. *See tour escort.*

tour escort. The person designated as the leader of a tour group responsible for travel arrangements throughout the trip.

tour guide. *See tour escort.*

tourist class. *See coach class.*

transfer. The transportation of a passenger from a carrier's terminal to a hotel or another point in the destination.

Transportation Security Administration (TSA). The U.S. agency created in 2001 to coordinate all homeland security functions for the federal government. It includes screenings at all U.S. commercial airports and seaports; affiliated agencies include the Coast Guard, Customs, and Bureau of Customs and Immigration Services.

travel advisory. An official notice from a government agency that a danger or hazard may exist for travelers going to a specific destination.

travel insurance. An insurance policy that provides protection for travelers, their possessions, and their trip deposits and payments in the event of unforeseen dangers or hazards that interfere with a trip.

travel warning. An official notice from a government agency that recommends that travelers avoid a specific destination based on actual dangers or hazards that exist.

trip cancellation insurance. A policy that protects travelers before a trip starts, reimbursing them for any prepaid travel expenses that cannot be refunded if they must cancel the trip.

trip interruption insurance. A policy that protects travelers during a trip, reimbursing them for travel expenses resulting from delays, changes, or the sudden end of the trip, as well as for injuries, accidents, or other events that cause them to change their itinerary once the trip is underway.

triple. A hotel room or cabin for three people.

twin. A room for two people with separate beds.

U

unaccompanied minor. A child (usually under the age of 18) traveling alone on an airplane with the prior approval of the airline.

unrestricted fare. A price that does not require advance purchase or other stipulations.

unscheduled. Not arranged in advance.

upgrade. To change to a better class of service.

utilization rate. The percentage of a car rental company's (or individual location's) vehicles in use during a specific period of time.

V

value added tax. A government-imposed tax on goods and services (usually refundable to travelers who are not citizens of the country charging the tax).

vicarious responsibility. Liability that a supervisory party bears for the actionable conduct of a subordinate, associate, or agent because of the relationship between the two parties.

visa. An entry in a passport made by a consular official of a government giving permission to the bearer to enter the country.

Visa Waiver Program. The U.S. federal program that allows travelers who are citizens of certain countries (notably Europe) to enter the United States without applying first for a visa.

voucher. A coupon to be exchanged for travel services proving prior payment for the services.

W

waitlist. A list established when there are no more available spaces or seats.

waiver. The intentional dismissal of a requirement, claim, or right.

walk-in. A traveler who did not make prior reservations before arriving.

walk-up. A traveler who purchases a ticket just before departure.

walked. The term used when a traveler arrives at a hotel with a reservation but no rooms are available, leading the hotel to pay for the traveler's room at another property.

warranty of fitness. An express or implied promise that the property or service in a contract is suitable for the particular purpose desired by the buyer.

warranty of safety. An express or implied promise that the property or service in a contract is safe for the purpose desired by the buyer.

weekend rate. A discounted price often used to attract leisure travelers to business hotels on weekends.

windward. The direction towards the wind.

Y

yield management. A pricing system that adjusts rates based on the expected and historical demand for the seats on a given flight, departure, or sailing.

young driver's fee. A charge imposed by a car rental company on renters who are younger than the company's minimum rental age.

appendix a:
Filing
Effective Complaint Letters

Because most travel-related complaints involve relatively small amounts of money—the cost of a discounted airline ticket or the charge for a two-night hotel stay, for example—you will almost always be faced with resolving travel disputes on your own rather than hiring an attorney. Many travel suppliers try to settle consumer complaints quickly and amicably because they understand the importance of a good reputation and repeat business. However, you will not be heard until you have presented your complaint to the supplier directly.

The first step in filing an effective complaint against a travel supplier is knowing your rights as a traveler. If you have read the sections of this book that cover your complaint and you still believe that you have a valid argument, then you should proceed.

By far, your best chances of complaining successfully will come when you talk to the supplier's representatives for an immediate solution. For example, if you arrive at a hotel to find that the property is oversold (even though you have a guaranteed reservation), you should always insist—politely, but firmly—that you will not leave the front desk until the hotel finds you a replacement room or arranges for you to be *walked* to a nicer property near the hotel. If you must wait until after the trip to file your complaint in writing, your chances of a happy resolution have dropped greatly.

When you write a complaint letter to a travel company, be firm, but polite in your tone. Enclose copies of any documentation that supports your claim, such as receipts, tickets, photos, confirmation notices, and other paperwork (never send the originals). If you are a repeat customer, mention in your letter how often you have used the company's travel services. Finally, spell out in the letter exactly what you want from the supplier—a replacement ticket, a refund, or other compensation—and include the date by which you expect to receive a reply.

Because travel company addresses change often, you should consult a respected travel industry reference such as the *Official Travel Industry Directory* (**www.otid.com**) to find the mailing address, phone number, fax number, or email address for the supplier you have targeted in your complaint.

Which company officials should receive your complaint letter? The best strategy is calling the supplier to ask for the name of the staffer who handles consumer complaints and for the name of the company president. Then, address the letter to the consumer complaints person, but send a copy addressed to the president.

If you do not receive a reply by the date specified in your letter, send a follow-up letter explaining your complaint and setting a second deadline for replies. Enclose a copy of your first letter, and send this packet to both the consumer complaints person and the president.

If the second letter passes with no response, consider sending a final letter threatening legal action (such as a small claims court filing) and copy the letter to the company's industry association (for example, the Association of Retail Travel Agents and the American Society of Travel Agents if you are complaining about your travel agent). You should also send a copy to local reporters, as well as national consumer advocates such as Clark Howard (**www.clarkhoward.com**), in hopes that they will address your complaint in a future story.

appendix b:
Travel Magazines
and Guidebooks

In today's world—filled with thousands of travel agencies and travel websites, as well as growing questions about terrorism and global economic woes—information is the traveling consumer's best friend. These travel magazines give you a thorough foundation in basic travel news and tips, while the recommended guidebooks can offer additional details about specific destinations and type of travel.

TRAVEL MAGAZINES

Arthur Frommer's Budget Travel—**www.frommers.com**
Very practical, money-saving tips for *real people*
10 issues per year

Condé Nast Traveler—**www.concierge.com/cntraveler**
Glossy travel narratives with a focus on *truth in travel*
12 issues per year

Cruise Travel—**http://cruisetravelmag.com**
Hands-on, detailed articles on all aspects of cruise vacations
6 issues per year

InsideFlyer—**www.insideflyer.com**
> Tips and strategies for travelers who want to maximize
> their frequent flier benefits
> 12 issues per year

Islands—**www.islands.com**
> Crisp photography and stories for *island travelers and
> dreamers*
> 8 issues per year

National Geographic Traveler—
www.nationalgeographic.com/traveler
> Excellent *travel experience* articles and photos with
> practical travel advice
> 8 issues per year

Porthole—**www.porthole.com**
> A *resource guide* to the world of cruising
> 6 issues per year

Travel 50 & Beyond—**www.travel50andbeyond.com**
> Vacation ideas and tips for travelers over fifty years of age
> 4 issues per year

Travel & Leisure—**www.travelandleisure.com**
> Upscale travel advice emphasizing the experience of
> the trip
> 12 issues per year

Additional publications that focus on specific destinations or types of trips can be found in the *Travel* section of:

www.magazines.com

www.magsonthenet.com

www.amazon.com

TRAVEL GUIDEBOOK SERIES

AAA (**www.aaa.com**) publishes more than 40 different titles on U.S. and international destinations—guidebooks that are long on contact details for hotels and other suppliers, but sometimes short on narrative descriptions.

The *Fodor's* (**www.fodors.com**) and *Frommer's* (**www.frommers.com**) series are the most comprehensive and thoroughly updated series of basic guidebooks, recommended as the basic reference titles for most U.S. and global destinations.

Insight Guidebooks (**www.insightguides.com**) feature local writers with incredible photography, relying more on essays than hotel listings to describe the destination.

The *Let's Go* series (**www.letsgo.com**) is written specifically for students traveling independently in other countries.

Lonely Planet (**www.lonelyplanet.com**) is the world's leading independent travel publisher, with 650 guidebooks in fourteen languages.

Avalon Travel Publishing (**www.travelmatters.com**) produces two popular series: the *Moon Handbooks* (**www.moon.com**) and Rick Steves' *Europe Through the Back Door* books (**www.ricksteves.com**).

Rough Guides (**www.roughguides.com**) are small, pocket-size texts that will come in handy if you want a street-ready reference without lugging around the larger guidebooks.

Index

About the Authors

Alexander Anolik, Esq. is president of the largest U.S. law corporation emphasizing the practice of travel law and travel industry litigation. From his San Francisco offices, he has represented thousands of traveling consumers, travel agents, travel suppliers, and government tourism offices throughout his career. His books include *The Law and the Travel Industry*, the first comprehensive travel law textbook, with a fifth edition scheduled for later in 2003.

Anolik co-founded the International Forum of Travel and Tourism Advocates (IFTTA), a global organization of travel industry attorneys, and served as IFTTA's president for seven years. He has conducted seminars throughout the world on travel, tourism, and hospitality law, as well as travel law classes at Cornell University, Golden Gate University, the University of Hawaii, and San Francisco State University.

Anolik serves as general counsel of the *Association of Retail Travel Agents*, the largest nonprofit trade association in North America that represents travel agents exclusively. He is co-editor of *IFTTA News*, a global newsletter for travel attorneys and the former travel law editor for *Travel Agent Magazine*. He has appeared regularly as a travel law commentator for ABC, CBS, CNN, NBC, MSNBC, CNBC, particularly the shows "48 Hours," "Inside Edition," and "Dateline."

Anolik earned his law degree from the University of California (Hastings College of the Law), with graduate legal studies at the University of California, Berkeley, School of Law (Boalt Hall) and at the Academia Internationalis Lex ex Scientia, The Hague, Netherlands. He is a member of the bar in California and the District of Columbia and is admitted to practice in several U.S. district courts, the U.S. Tax Court, and the U.S. Supreme Court.

John K. Hawks is Executive Director of the Consumer Travel Rights Center (**www.mytravelrights.com**), the largest U.S. nonprofit group dedicated solely to defending and expanding the legal rights of travelers.

He serves also as president of the *Association of Retail Travel Agents*. He has written several books on travel and tourism issues, including *Career Opportunities in Travel and Tourism* and *Youth Exchanges: The Complete Guide to the Homestay Experience Abroad*— both published by Facts on File.

He currently resides in Lexington, KY.